THE POWER OF PYRUVATE

THE POWER OF PYRUVATE

The Natural Way to Better Health and Well-Being

Ronald T. Stanko, M.D.
with Laura O'Hare

KEATS PUBLISHING

LOS ANGELES

NTC/Contemporary Publishing Group

Library of Congress Cataloging-in-Publication Data

Stanko, Ronald T.
　　The power of pyruvate : the natural way to better health and well-being /
Ronald T. Stanko with Laura O'Hare
　　　　p.　cm.
　　Includes bibliographical references and index.
　　ISBN 0-87983-990-2
　　1. Pyruvic acid— health aspects I. O'Hare, Laura II. Title.
QPB801.P86S73　　1999
612'.0517—dc21　　　　　　　　　　　　　　　　　　　99-31539
　　　　　　　　　　　　　　　　　　　　　　　　　　　　　CIP

Published by Keats Publishing
A division of NTC/Contemporary Publishing Group, Inc.
4255 West Touhy Avenue, Lincolnwood, Illinois 60646-1975 U.S.A.

Design and typography by Type Shoppe II Productions Ltd. of Chestertown, Maryland

Printed in the United States of America

International Standard Book Number: 0-87983-990-2

99 00 01 02 03 04 VP 18 17 16 15 14 13 12 11 10 9 8 7 6 5 4 3 2 1

CONTENTS

INTRODUCTION

Would you like to influence fat metabolism in such a way that you could decrease body fat and body weight without losing muscle? Would you like to increase your exercise capacity by at least 20 percent? To protect your heart from damage while increasing its efficiency? To thwart the production of free radicals that are now known to be culprits in many of our most dreaded diseases? Would you like to protect your DNA? To inhibit cancer growth? To sleep more soundly? If so, read on and join us in discovering the power of pyruvate, a natural way to better health and well-being.

Twenty-five years ago, my colleagues and I began our research about pyruvic acid compounds, or *pyruvate*—natural compounds that are always present in the body and diet. What we discovered amazed us, and we think it will amaze you. But first you must understand what pyruvate is.

What Is Pyruvate?

Pyruvate is a natural, three-carbon compound that is found in the body at all times (Figure 1).

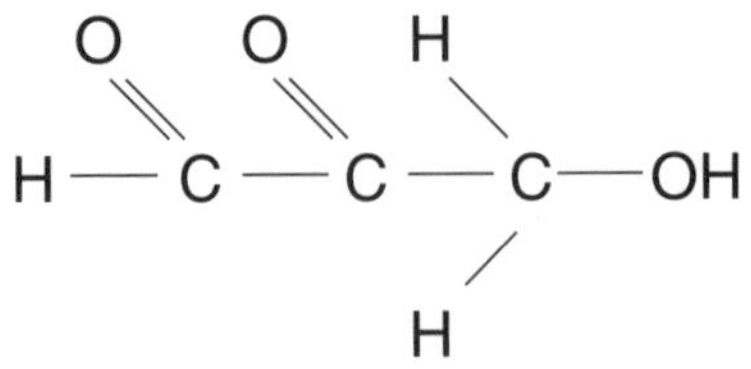

$$\underset{\displaystyle H}{\overset{\displaystyle O \quad\quad O \quad\quad H}{H - C - C - C - OH}}$$

Figure 1. *Chemical makeup of pyruvate.*

It is a breakdown product of the six-carbon compound glucose. Glucose is a carbohydrate, one of the most common of the human body's fuels. In fact, carbohydrates are found in most of the foods we eat. The metabolism of glucose, a process called *glycolysis*, almost always produces pyruvate as well as energy to be used or stored (Figure 2).

Once pyruvate is formed, it goes to work immediately by entering the mitochondria, where it creates energy. The mitochondrion is a component of most living cells. The body makes energy in the mitochondria, primarily from the food we eat. Pyruvate is the main compound that can freely enter the mitochondria; any other compound is usually broken down into pyruvate before it can gain admittance to the mitochondria. Glucose, for example, usually will just sit outside the mitochondria's cellular walls, unable in its six-carbon form to feed the mitochondria's energy furnace. But when glucose is broken down into pyruvate, these walls no longer present a barrier.

An Apple a Day

Pyruvate is found in red apples, red wine, and certain cheeses (see "Pyruvate in Foods" on page 125, which may account for the old saying "An apple a day keeps the doctor away." Pyruvate could also be the reason for the somewhat surprising recent finding that the typical French diet, which is high in the consumption of both cheese and red wine (neither of which we usually think of as particularly healthy) has resulted in a lower rate of heart disease in

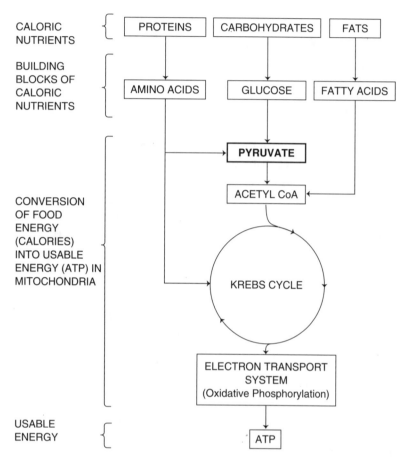

Figure 2. *The central role of pyruvate in metabolism.*

France than we have in the United States, in spite of equal amounts of dietary fat consumption. Pyruvate is also found in most fruits and vegetables, which could shed light on the inexplicable fact that greater consumption of fruits and vegetables is consistently linked to the reduction of chronic diseases such as heart disease and cancer. Pyruvate used in animal studies has been remarkably successful in both the treatment of and the prevention of ischemic organ damage, such as heart and intestinal disease. Pyruvate has been shown to have a positive impact on other diseases that have been linked to dietary content, including cancer.

So, if we already have pyruvate in our system and it's found in our diet, why should we take more of it? And if we do, why will it make a difference?

More of a Good Thing

For a long time, scientists did not quite know what to do with pyruvate; nor did they consider it really worth pursuing. Although we thought it was an intriguing compound that could likely affect metabolism, we got no effect when we studied it in the dosage already found in the diet (approximately 1 gram). Most scientists didn't consider administering it in dosages higher than those usually found in the diet or the human body because of a generally accepted notion at the time known as *product inhibition theory*.

Product Inhibition Theory

Product inhibition is best explained by starting with the simple diagram shown in Figure 3:

COMPOUND 1 $\longrightarrow$ ENZYME $\longrightarrow$ COMPOUND 2

Figure 3. *Metabolizing compounds.*

In the above figure, compound 1 breaks down into compound 2 until a given amount of compound 2 is produced. Once that given amount of compound 2 is produced, the reaction slows or stops. Beyond that, no matter how much compound 1 is added to the mix, it will not be metabolized into compound 2. This is because the body has a set amount of compound 2 that the body requires to function, and so the body will not continue the breakdown process once that level of compound has been achieved. Further, if the body receives from an outside source an equivalent or greater amount of the compound than it normally metabolizes on its own, the body will usually slow the metabolism (or creation) of said compound. Thus, to introduce greater quantities of compounds regularly found in the human body at set levels may seem pointless, because they would not be metabolized or absorbed, nor would a concentration be built up in the body. Quite a lot of data suggested that this product inhibition theory was generally applicable to compounds found in the human body.

What does this mean in terms of pyruvate consumption? Based on product inhibition theory, it would be useless to take 5 grams of pyruvate if your body normally metabolized only 1 gram, because the body would simply dispose of the excess. It turns out that compound inhibition theory does apply to many of the compounds found in the body, but pyruvate isn't one of them.

Pyruvate: Overwhelming Inhibition

When I began to study pyruvate, I hypothesized that pyruvate would overwhelm the end product inhibition theory (Figure 4).

PDH

PYRUVATE $\longrightarrow$ COMPOUND 2, MITOCHONDRIAL FUNCTION, ETC.

Figure 4. *Metabolizing pyruvate.*

I felt that because of the peculiarity of pyruvate dehydrogenase (PDH)—the enzyme involved in pyruvate metabolism—increasing amounts of pyruvate (compound 1) would continue the breakdown into compound 2, stimulate metabolism and the mitochondria, and induce benefits. This concept has been subsequently pursued by other researchers who have spent their entire professional lives evaluating the metabolic effects of pyruvate. They have determined that, contrary to what most people assumed, an increase in pyruvate availability to the body does not necessarily shut down PDH and the body's metabolism of pyruvate, or subsequent mitochondrial function (Mallet and Bunger 1993). In fact, the reverse is true. The greater the concentration of pyruvate, the more quickly it enters the cell, unlike glucose and most other body fuels (Behal et al. 1993).

The original pyruvate hypothesis clearly is correct. Pyruvate's ability to enter cells and the mitochondria at higher concentrations may very well be pyruvate's primary benefit to the body. This fact reminds us of the necessity of scientifically evaluating any hypothesis, no matter how greatly it differs from the general beliefs of the day.

How Much Is Enough?

So if an increased dosage is what's needed to reveal pyruvate's terrific benefits, the next question is, of course, How much of an increase? Is there a "magic amount"? It turns out that there is, and it was determined by comparing my data with data of other researchers in the United States and Europe.

Give Me 5!

The normal amount of pyruvate found in the diet is equivalent to the intake of about 0.5 to 1 gram per day. This results in a concentration of pyruvate in the cells in the amount of approximately $1/2$ millimole, where millimole is simply a scientific measure of concentration. As the intake of pyruvate increases, the level of pyruvate in the blood increases; interestingly, as quickly as the blood level increases, pyruvate enters into the cell. When pyruvate enters the cell at high concentrations, good things happen. As you ingest about 2 grams of pyruvate per day, you'll probably get a cellular concentration of approximately 2 millimoles, and the positive results begin to be seen, reaching their peak when the cellular concentration is at 4 to 5 millimoles (Yanos, Patti, and Stanko 1994). This happens when approximately 4 to 5 grams of pyruvate are ingested per day.

Happily, these benefits are totally natural. Increasing pyruvate concentration only stimulates normal metabolism, and no toxic by-product is created.

How We Got Here

As I've said, scientists have been looking at pyruvate for some time. But its real potential was envisioned seriously for the first time during the late 1960s and early 1970s by three of us who lived on different continents and had no idea that we were thinking the same thing at the same time!

In England, during the late 1960s, Lord Butterfield of Cambridge University was working with different drugs and compounds in an attempt to improve and control diabetes. In looking at the pathway of glucose metabolism, he determined that pyruvate might be beneficial in the treatment of diabetes. This proved to be correct. Unfortunately, Lord Butterfield's administrative duties prevented him from proceeding with much more research, but he never abandoned his belief in this theory of pyruvate's potential benefit.

At the same time, Rolf Bunger, a young researcher in Germany, learned about pyruvate from a senior research scientist who was researching what was then a hypothesis: that pyruvate, being the center of glycolysis, might be able to manipulate metabolism in a beneficial way. Specifically, he believed that pyruvate might benefit the heart. Inspired by this research, Dr. Bunger moved to the United States, where he continued the research and became convinced of pyruvate's benefits.

Meanwhile, as a young medical student, I had been assigned as a project the task of designing a product that would benefit a great number of people. I chose to explore ways to help those with alcoholism, and I looked at the effect of alcohol on the process of glycolysis. At that time, it was believed that alcohol impeded glycolysis and therefore energy production, resulting in liver disease as well as the skinny and amuscular condition common to many alcoholics. I theorized that if you could stimulate glycolysis, and thus energy production, through pyruvate supplementation, these conditions could be positively impacted. My research into the benefits of pyruvate began with this student project, but it wasn't until the 1990s that Dr. Bunger and I decided to coordinate our research. Lord Dr. Butterfield and I didn't meet until the early 1990s.

Lots of Benefits

When you look at the list of pyruvate's beneficial properties, it probably seems a little too good to be true. If I were seeing it for the first time, I undoubtedly would feel the same way. When I started the pyruvate research, I never imagined, nor could I foresee, such a lengthy index of potential benefits. As you'll see when you read further, one discovery snowballed into another. Each new discovery stimulated another, and each benefit could be linked to others—not an uncommon scenario in a good scientific investigation. Here's the current list of potential pyruvate benefits:

1. Enhancement of fat loss and weight loss with weight reduction therapy
2. Prevention of fat gain and weight gain with overeating
3. Enhancement of exercise capacity
4. Inhibition of production of free radicals. Free radicals have been implicated as damaging agents in many diverse diseases such as cancer, heart disease, and arthritis
5. Scavenging of free radicals
6. Inhibition of cancer growth
7. Inhibition of ischemic heart injury
8. Inhibition of ischemic intestinal injury
9. Decrease in heart damage after heart attack
10. Decrease in blood cholesterol with consumption of a high-fat diet
11. Increase in heart muscle efficiency (the heart is able to pump blood without needing or using as much oxygen)
12. Decrease in blood glucose in diabetes
13. Decrease in diabetic eye disease
14. Increase in cellular energy
15. Inhibition of cell death
16. Prevention of DNA damage
17. Inhibition of injury to transplanted organs
18. Inhibition of injury to organs being readied for transplant while outside the body

There is more to come as the development of pyruvate continues.

Twenty-Five Years in the Making

If I thought that pyruvate could do so many good things for so many people twenty-five years ago, why haven't I gone to the general public with my findings before now? There are several reasons.

First, pyruvate's benefits were mostly theoretical at that time. Although I was able to prove some on my own, little is accepted in the eyes of the scientific community until it's been found in independent research studies. So although my hypotheses were interesting, they were unproved.

Second, it wasn't enough for me to satisfy the scientific community, the Food and Drug Administration (FDA), or anybody else. I had to satisfy the toughest critic of all: myself. As a physician and researcher, I didn't want to release my findings until I was absolutely sure of them. Although there are more than forty published manuscripts in medical journals documenting pyruvate research, I purposely kept the media out of any of my seminars or presentations in which the benefits of pyruvate were discussed. It was important to me that when the public became aware of the benefits of pyruvate, many other scientifically sound studies would also identify such benefits. For example, years of research had convinced me that pyruvate could have truly meaningful health benefits, and one of those benefits is the aid in weight loss. Mishandled, this kind of information could turn my twenty-five years of research into the "hype" or "sensationalistic" publicity I have worked hard to avoid. I didn't want pyruvate to have fifteen minutes of fame and then fizzle because I could not defend my claims. I wanted to be sure that it truly worked before offering the potential benefits to the public. I waited to release any information on pyruvate until now because I wanted to be able to explain and back up these data.

Third, until the Congressional Dietary Supplement Act was passed in 1994, pyruvate—although a natural compound found in the body at all times—was subject to drug approval by the FDA. And it had, for at least ten years, been proving itself under the strict scrutiny of FDA drug trials. However, under this new law, if a natural compound has been researched and those researchers have published peer-reviewed medical studies to attest to its benefits and its lack of harmful effects, then that compound can be marketed without FDA drug approval. The effects of pyruvate have been documented in prestigious medical journals such as *Metabolism, American Journal of Physiology, Journal of Applied Physiology,* and the *American Journal of Clinical Nutrition.*

Pyruvate can be rightly categorized as a dietary supplement, not a drug. And thanks to Congress, it can now be made available inexpensively, without a prescription, to people it might really help.

Now, as I do throughout this book, I end this chapter with some questions and answers that reflect a range of inquiries that I have been asked to address.

Q & A: Introduction to Pyruvate

? *What is the effective dosage of pyruvate?*

The benefits of pyruvate begin to be seen at a dosage of 2 to 3 grams per day and are greatest at 4 to 5 grams per day. As with many substances, effectiveness varies with the size and weight of the consumer. In other words, an 80-pound woman may well achieve a benefit ingesting less than the dose for a 280-pound wrestler. We recommend 3 to 4 grams daily for the smaller person and a maximum of 4 to 5 grams daily for the larger person. You won't get a druglike high from pyruvate. You won't "feel" its effect on body fat and metabolism. After a few days of taking pyruvate, you may be able to run a little farther, but that increased ability won't be accompanied by a steroid or amphetaminelike high. Nor will you feel a "burst" of energy per se. You simply will start running and will be able to run farther; and when your run is over, you'll be pleasantly surprised to discover how much farther you've gone and a little baffled as to how you were able to do it. Just accept it.

? *If 5 grams is good, is 10 grams better?*

It is doubtful. The benefits of pyruvate seem to level out at about 5 to 6 grams per day. You will not get twice the effect by taking 10 grams instead of 5 grams. The excess probably won't hurt you, and I know some of you are going to try higher doses. But I have found nothing to suggest that a dosage of more than 5 grams is worth either the effort or the money.

? *Should you take pyruvate forever?*

Again, as with any other substance, it is probably not good to take something at therapeutic doses everyday forever. I believe the best regimen would be to take pyruvate at therapeutic doses for eight to ten weeks, decrease the dose for one or two weeks, and begin high doses again. This dosage schedule is not uncommon in the practice of medicine for long-term therapies. But as you will see later in the book, many of the benefits of pyruvate will be preventive, and I strongly recommend consistent long-term use. Speaking of preventive uses, you obviously can't feel a prevention. What I mean is, you may well get benefits from pyruvate that you'll never be aware of. For instance, if you're trying to prevent the complications of diabetes, and you succeed, you'll have no way of knowing whether it was the pyruvate that did it for you. In another twenty-five years, scientists might be able to say with reasonable certainty that, yes, had you not taken pyruvate, you would indeed have suffered the expected complications of diabetes. All you'll ever know is that, for whatever reasons, you were better off. Of course, this means pyruvate may not always get the credit it so greatly deserves, but that's a concern I'll happily face if it means better health for you.

? *Can children take pyruvate?*

Yes, but this is a qualified yes. Obviously, when children take pyruvate, the dose has to be smaller, probably no more than 1 to 2 grams per day. We don't recommend that children take an adult dose. I see no problem, however, with children ingesting liquid drinks, or food bars, containing small amounts of pyruvate. That's as safe as eating an apple, which contains almost $1/2$ gram of pyruvate, or a banana, which contains almost 0.1 gram of pyruvate. It is doubtful that eating two to four apples per day, along with a banana or two, could ever harm a child.

Concerning weight control in children, a recent study indicates that overweight children from ten to seventeen years old who have overweight parents tend to be overweight as adults (Whitaker et al. 1997). If we are to prevent adulthood obesity, treatment of certain adolescents is imperative. I think pyruvate would certainly be beneficial in weight control of adolescents. In the obese child or teenager, who obviously has more fat synthesis (fat formation) and/or less fat oxidation (fat breakdown), major benefits would be expected with consumption of higher doses of pyruvate. Thus a higher dose of pyruvate might be indicated than would normally be given to a person in this age group.

? *Can pregnant women take pyruvate?*

I would say no. The effects of pyruvate on a growing fetus are unknown. May I add, this doesn't apply just to pyruvate: When one is pregnant, any compound or supplement that hasn't been proved safe for a fetus should be avoided.

? *Don't pregnant women eat fruits and vegetables containing pyruvate without harm to the baby?*

Yes, and it is possible that pyruvate does fetuses no harm. Someday we might learn it will benefit them. But until I know, I insist on following the creed of doctors and scientists everywhere: "Do no harm while trying to do good." This recommendation might sound too conservative to some, but I would rather be very conservative than very wrong.

? *If you're taking pyruvate to combat obesity, will it also help the heart?*

Aside from the fact that losing excess weight is good for anybody's heart, the answer is yes, but yes with an explanation. Individually marketed pyruvate products will have other components specific to a given benefit. For instance, exercise products will contain more sodium than obesity products, as well as other constituents specific for exercise. The heart product will have other constituents shown to be beneficial to the heart. So, in order to maximize your benefits, be sure to buy the pyruvate product most suitable to your needs.

THE POWER OF PYRUVATE

Chapter 1

Weight Loss: The Never-Ending Search to Control Body Fat

Of the many benefits of pyruvate, its ability to aid in the loss of body fat and weight will undoubtedly be among the most popular. When used in conjunction with a reasonable diet and exercise, pyruvate may be a key factor in impeding the onset of "middle-age spread" and may help prevent the development of obesity so common in industrialized societies.

Body fat and weight content depend on several things:

1. How many calories go into your body (what you eat)
2. What happens to those calories in your body (metabolism)
3. How many calories you expend by daily living (expenditure and exercise)

We all know how difficult it is to completely control the amount we eat. Certainly, any program of dietary restriction can and should control weight and obesity. But how successful are these programs? Exercise increases caloric expenditure and enhances the loss of calories. However, despite the overwhelming public interest in exercise programs, many people have neither the time nor the desire to exercise. Although I strongly believe in, and highly recommend, dietary control and exercise, the incidence of overweight and obesity would be much lower if diet and exercise guidelines were easy to follow.

Manipulating a person's metabolism to control fat metabolism and weight, obesity, or disease is not a new idea. It was popular in the 1950s at many prestigious academic institutions. The strategy has been to manipulate metabolism with drugs or compounds foreign to the human body. Although potentially effective, these substances frequently have negative side effects. Remember amphetamines and fen-phen? They were effective but also very dangerous, and are now tightly controlled substances. In contrast, natural compounds such as pyruvate affect fat metabolism without the risk of using drugs or compounds foreign to the human body.

My initial studies to determine whether pyruvate could aid in the inhibition of fat production had nothing to do with weight control. I was attempting to impede the onset of "fatty liver," a condition of fat deposits in the livers of people who drink excessively that usually occurs before the onset of cirrhosis.

Fatty liver, in and of itself, is not particularly problematic and does not necessarily lead to cirrhosis. Cirrhosis is, however, usually preceded by fatty liver. My question was this: By administering pyruvate, could fatty liver be prevented, and in so doing prevent, or at least impede, the onset of cirrhosis? I began the research, using rodents as my experimental subjects. Those first studies were successful; pyruvate supplements did indeed impede fat production in animal livers (Stanko et al. 1978).

If We Could Make a Rodent's Liver Leaner, Why Not Its Abdomen as Well?

Having proved what I set out to in terms of liver fat production, I began to address another very interesting result of our research: Along with a decrease in the rodent's liver fat came a decrease in its abdominal fat. If pyruvate could impede fat production in the liver and the stomach, it seemed only logical that it could have the same effect throughout the body. My research team and I set out to prove it.

In research studies that were repeated many times, we separated healthy male rodents of a normal weight into two groups. Each group was fed the same diet and kept under the same conditions, but only one group was given the pyruvate supplement.

At the end of the studies, the rodents' body composition was analyzed. What we found was this:

1. Rodents who took the pyruvate supplement gained less weight than those who didn't.
2. Rodents who took the pyruvate supplement had a 32 percent smaller fat content than the rats who didn't.
3. There was little difference in the protein or water content of the pyruvate animals as opposed to that of the control animals. In other words, weight loss could be attributed not to loss of water or loss of muscle mass, but to inhibition of fat (lipid) production. (Stanko and Adibi 1986)

So, in a normal, healthy rodent, pyruvate could promote the reduction of body fat and inhibit weight gain. Now it was time to see how a fat animal might benefit.

New Hope for Fat Rodents

The next study, performed at the University of Texas at Austin by John Ivy, Ph.D., was with Zucker rodents, a breed that is genetically obese and commonly studied as a model for obesity. Along with obesity, the rodents commonly have a low resting metabolic rate (rate of energy expenditure).

Dr. Ivy studied two groups of obese animals. Both were fed identical calories, but one group was supplemented with pyruvate and the other with a placebo (glucose).

After five weeks, body analysis of these animals provided more promising results. Those rodents fed pyruvate showed an increased expenditure of resting energy, along with increased oxidation or "burning" of fat, while their weight and food conversion efficiency (the conversion of food calories to fat and weight) was reduced (Figure 1.1) (Cortez et al. 1991).

Now that we knew that pyruvate could help rodents reduce body fat, we decided to go to Montana and do the same for swine.

This Little Piggy Trimmed Down

Since downtown Pittsburgh is not particularly conducive to the housing of pigs, I conducted this next phase of the research at Montana State University with the help of Walt and Rosemary Newman, a husband-and-wife team, each having a Ph.D. in animal science and nutrition.

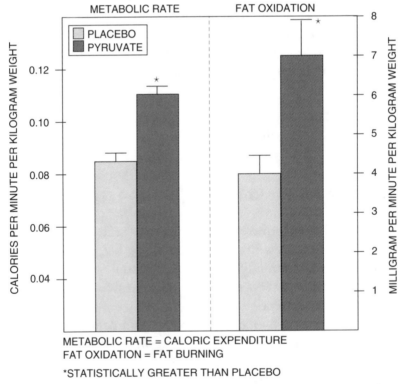

METABOLIC RATE = CALORIC EXPENDITURE
FAT OXIDATION = FAT BURNING

*STATISTICALLY GREATER THAN PLACEBO

Figure 1.1. *Metabolic rate and oxidation in obese rodents: pyruvate or placebo.*

Source: M. Y. Cortez, C. E. Torgan, J. T. Brozinick Jr., R. H. Miller, and J. L. Ivy, "Effects of pyruvate and dihydroxyacetone on the growth and metabolic state of obese Zucker rats," *American Journal of Clinical Nutrition* 53 (1991): 847–53.

While our primary interest was in discovering pyruvate's direct benefits for humans, fat reduction in swine has obvious interest for pig farmers as well, namely, leaner pork for a calorie-conscious consumer. The Newmans set up experimental groups of pigs from the same litters, all of which were fed the same feed, some with the addition of pyruvate, others with the addition of placebo.

At the end of the study, the Newmans determined that pyruvate had again acted to impede fat production. The pork loins and legs from the pyruvate-fed swine were 12 to 15 percent less fatty than those of the placebo group. The protein mass in both groups remained basically equal (Stanko et al. 1989). Thus we had identified another species in which pyruvate could decrease body fat. After these many successful studies in animal models, it was time to go on to the next level of study—human trials.

Human Clinical Research (or, Forty-Four Really Good Sports)

I could not have advanced in my research without the help of forty-four very generous women. All were overweight, and each participated in one of three studies. They agreed to walk away from their lives and live in our clinic for periods of time ranging from three to six weeks, restricted to bed except for walks to the lavatory or kitchen. They ate only the controlled diet we fed them, and they endured constant monitoring during their stay with us. For this, we thank them.

Our first study involved fourteen women. Their average age was in the middle forties. To estimate their body composition, we determined conductance through the body. With the help of certain equations we could measure body fat content. Body fat distribution was characterized by estimating fat deposits at the waist and hips. Resting metabolic rate was measured by using a portable metabolic cart.

The women were divided into two groups. One-half were given a pyruvate supplement, and one-half were given a placebo. Both groups were fed a low-energy diet of 1000 calories per day. Twenty-one days later, we were ready to analyze the results.

The weight loss of the women who were given pyruvate increased by 37 percent compared to those who were not given pyruvate. Their fat loss was 48 percent higher than that of the women given the placebo. Their resting metabolic rates, however, remained essentially the same, as did their heart, liver, and thyroid functions and their body protein (or muscle) loss (Figure 1.2) (Stanko, Tietze, and Arch 1992*a*).

The gracious subjects of this study will be able to enjoy the fruits of their labors. With their help, we have come to the conclusion that supplementing a low-energy but mildly restricted weight loss diet with a certain amount of pyruvate will increase fat loss and weight loss.

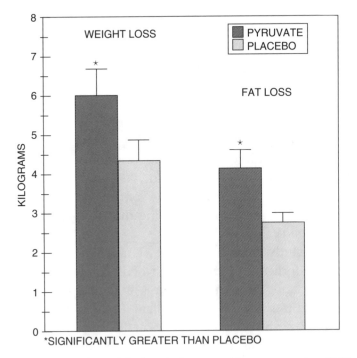

Figure 1.2. *Body weight and fat loss in human subjects consuming 1000-calorie diets.*

Source: R. T. Stanko, D. L. Tietze, and J. E. Arch, "Body composition, energy utilization, and nitrogen metabolism with a 4.25 MJ/d low-energy diet supplemented with pyruvate," *American Journal of Clinical Nutrition* 56 (1992a): 630–35.

We then moved on to see if pyruvate could be helpful with a more severely restricted diet. A new group of women, thirteen in number, were admitted to our clinic under the same medical guidelines as the first group. Their body mass was measured in the same fashion, and their daily routine was under the same restrictions.

The difference was this: These women were given a severely restricted diet of only 500 calories per day. All women, as expected, lost weight and body fat; but our results were, again, what we'd expected. In the group fed the pyruvate supplement, weight loss was improved by 16 percent and fat loss by 23 percent, compared to those who had been given the placebo (glucose) (Figure 1.3) (Stanko, Tietze, and Arch 1992*b*).

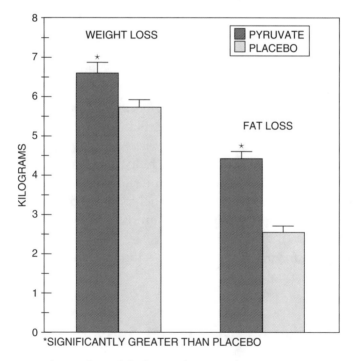

Figure 1.3. *Body weight and fat loss in human subjects consuming 500-calorie diets.*

Source: R. T. Stanko, D. L. Tietze, and J. E. Arch, "Body composition, energy utilization, and nitrogen metabolism with a severely restricted diet supplemented with dihydroxyacetone and pyruvate," *American Journal of Clinical Nutrition* 55 (1992*b*): 771–76.

Gone Today, Gone Tomorrow?

Numerous studies have shown that obese patients lose weight when they follow weight reduction diets, but unfortunately they gain much of it back when they resume their usual eating. I decided to see if pyruvate could alter that pattern.

In this final study, seventeen women were engaged. For twenty-one days, they ate a 300-calorie, hypoenergetic weight loss diet of fruits, vegetables, and eggs, resulting in the expected similar weight loss among the subjects. (All 300-calorie diets induce weight loss.) Then we took them off their diets and evaluated what happened as they overate and regained weight.

The women were divided into two groups, each receiving a moderately high calorie "overeating" weight gain diet. One-half were given a placebo with their food, while one-half received pyruvate supplement for another twenty-one days. The women put up with our restrictions and weight monitoring and testing of body composition that enabled us to make a very exciting discovery.

Remarkably, while eating a diet designed to cause weight gain, the subjects who received pyruvate gained 36 percent less weight and 55 percent less body fat than their placebo-receiving counterparts without any significant loss of body protein (Stanko and Arch 1996). Pyruvate not only helped in the loss of fat and body weight with low-calorie diet therapy but also helped with the biggest problem of all: Pyruvate helped keep our subjects from gaining back weight when they were off the weight reduction diets (Figure 1.4).

So much for the studies. Now it's time to talk about what this might mean for you.

Pyruvate Takes on "Middle-Age Spread"

To best understand how pyruvate can help those of us not involved in clinical research trials to lose weight and keep it off, let's start at the beginning, specifically with how we put on weight. To do that, I'll create two imaginary couples: couple 1 and couple 2.

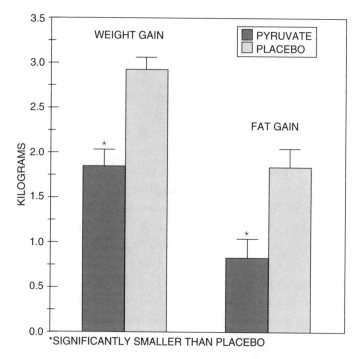

Figure 1.4. *Body weight and fat gain with refeeding after weight reduction.*

Source: R. T. Stanko and J. E. Arch, "Inhibition of regain in body weight and fat with addition of 3-carbon compounds to the diet with hyperenergetic feeding after weight reduction," *International Journal of Obesity* 20 (1996): 925–30.

Our imaginary couples are the same age, come from the same background, and have achieved the same level of education and financial stability. Both married right after college, and both couples were fit and healthy when they did so. However, when we meet them fifteen years later at their class reunion, we see there is now a marked difference between the two pairs. Couple 1 still fit into their wedding clothes. Couple 2 have each put on 30 pounds since they were married, and have developed "middle-age spread." What happened?

Weight gain with age (middle-age spread) is caused by

1. Decreased exercise—not uncommon as work and parenting take up more and more time
2. Decreased metabolic rate—small decrease with age, but still there

3. Decreased burning of fat—nicely documented in a recent study (Melanson et al. 1997)
4. Slight overeating—not massive overeating

Did couple 1 spend these years devoted to diet and fitness, while couple 2 did nothing more than lift a TV remote control with one hand and a slice of pizza with the other? Not at all. The noticeable difference in size between these two couples is actually attributable to years of tiny differences: a lifestyle that includes an extra mile or two of walking during the day, or one or two fewer cheeseburger-and-fries platters or desserts per week.

For most of us, weight gain sneaks up. Let's assume you are able to maintain your weight while eating a reasonable diet with a weekly splurge of a pizza, or cheeseburger, or ice cream sundae. If all you did was go from one weekly splurge to two, adding the equivalent of 150 to 250 calories per day more than necessary to maintain your weight, over time you would begin to add a pound or two. The same thing would happen if you eliminated exercise without an equivalent reduction in calories. If you eliminate the walking and add the cheeseburger or dessert, it makes sense that any weight gain can be quicker and greater.

Now we go back to our couples. Much about their lifestyles is similar. However, a close examination of their schedules reveals the differences that have, literally, added up.

Couple 1 exercise faithfully, at least sixty minutes, two to three days per week. Couple 2 exercise just thirty minutes, maybe one day a week, if it all. Couple 1 play backyard football with their kids; couple 2 watches football with theirs. Couple 1 walks from hole to hole when they golf; couple 2 rides the golf cart. Couple 1 prepares a gourmet, low-fat meal at home once per week; the rest of the time they watch their fat intake and avoid dessert. Couple 2 prepares fatty meats, homemade potato salad, and chocolate cake à la mode at least once a week, and they almost always have dessert.

Couple 2 puts on a pound here and there, and accepts it as the inevitable effect of getting older. Besides, what's a pound here or there? Well, at only 2 pounds per year, it's 30 pounds when class reunion time comes around.

So what does this have to do with pyruvate? Well, as you saw from our studies, supplementing with pyruvate increases the calorie- and fat-losing capabilities of even the most sedentary body—not by a huge amount but perhaps by 400 or 500 calories per day. But, as we've said, 400 or 500 calories per day could have stopped couple 2 from gaining those 30 pounds over the years by either slowing the creation of fat or increasing the destruction of fat.

However, pyruvate supplementation is not a license to go crazy. It won't protect you from a sedentary lifestyle and a daily relationship with a box of peanut brittle and pie à la mode. What it will do is help to even the playing field in the battle against the slight, natural slowing down of the metabolism as we age, along with the dietary and lifestyle changes common to aging.

I've Spread. Now What?

The same properties that make pyruvate so useful in maintaining a more attractive figure can also help you return to it. But in this fat and weight loss scenario, pyruvate probably can't do it alone. If you have 80 pounds to lose, a reduced-calorie diet and increased exercise are likely going to be necessary. But pyruvate can certainly help the process by increasing your capability for eliminating fat and maintaining protein (muscle) mass. Our research proved that pyruvate definitely increases fat loss and weight loss with weight reduction low-calorie diets. There are also benefits of increased energy, but we talk about that in another chapter.

These Pants Fit Now, But Next Week . . . ?

Finally, let's discuss keeping the weight off. Because our bodies appreciate a status quo, they quickly adjust to the reduced calories consumed during a diet. Metabolism slows. Because the body can quickly learn to maintain itself on fewer calories, most dieters hit the ever-dreaded plateaus. Since most of us can only reduce our intake of calories to a certain point, and for a certain period of time, we need something to increase our body's calorie-burning, or fat-burning, ability. Exercise is one approach. Now we also have pyruvate. Better still, they make great partners.

When you stop dieting, you probably keep that slightly slowed-down metabolism for awhile. Therefore, you can actually start regaining weight while eating a diet that before would have been fine for maintaining weight. Pyruvate helps compensate by picking up a little metabolic slack. So, if you eat 1800 calories along with pyruvate supplement, your body might read just 1500 calories—the amount your metabolism can handle to maintain your postdiet weight, or to lose more fat and weight!

Pyruvate: A Weight Control Team Player

Another terrific fact about pyruvate is that it can be used in conjunction with any diet and exercise plan that works for you. Jenny Craig or Weight Watchers, aerobics or the treadmill, vegetarian or high-protein diets—pyruvate can work right along with it to optimize your fat loss and weight loss efforts. In fact, for those who need to lose quite a bit of fat and weight, the greatest effects of pyruvate will be seen in conjunction with a lower-calorie diet.

If your weight loss plan includes an appetite suppressant, pyruvate might work with that, too. The big difference between the two is that appetite suppressants do just that, chemically suppress appetite, whereas pyruvate works naturally to help eliminate calories you do consume and the fat that might be made from those calories. Since pyruvate already occurs naturally in foods we eat as well as within our own bodies, there should be no problem with interaction.

Pyruvate makes weight reduction diets more efficacious, which is fantastic for the overweight. Beyond that, I am well aware that there are major problems involved in inhibiting weight regain after dieting and weight loss. I am reassured by our research, which shows that pyruvate will address that problem also. I agree completely with national experts that the control of obesity is best addressed by preventing it in the normal, or slightly overweight, person. It is exciting to know that pyruvate will inhibit fat gain and weight gain due to overeating, and pyruvate should be an ideal agent for the prevention of overweight and obesity.

Pyruvate should help keep you from putting on fat and weight. If you already are overweight, pyruvate helps you to take off fat and weight. After that, pyruvate will help you to maintain this fat loss and weight loss.

Q & A: Fat Loss and Weight Loss

? *Can pyruvate guarantee fat loss and weight loss?*

Nothing that is nontoxic can guarantee fat loss and weight loss. Many variables contribute to weight loss, which explains why some people can consume quite a few calories without gaining much, while others find they can barely eat without seeing the effects. On average, our research showed pyruvate to have positive benefits in aiding with fat loss and weight loss. Pyruvate is one of the first safe, scientifically evaluated natural compounds that should help with fat and weight control.

? *What's the difference between obesity and morbid obesity?*

Morbid obesity is defined as 100 pounds above ideal body weight. *Obesity* is defined as 25 to 30 pounds above ideal body weight; consequently, some people who might see themselves as having middle-age spread would actually be considered obese. Using the new body mass index (BMI) (height in meters divided by weight in kilograms) tables, some people (those whose BMI is greater than 25) would be considered overweight and others (those whose BMI is 30 or greater) would be considered obese. In the category of overweight (BMI of 25 to 30), those men who have a waist size greater than 40 inches, and those women who have a waist size greater than 35 inches, are considered susceptible to obesity-related diseases.

Why were the women kept so restricted during the obesity studies? Would pyruvate only help when taken under such strict guidelines?

In answer to the first question, the women were monitored so carefully in order to eliminate any variables which might affect the study. Even a few blocks of walking, or a tiny discrepancy in calorie intake, could cause me and everyone else to question the veracity of our findings. In answer to the second question, no—the restrictions were simply a standard for our study, not a means of maximizing pyruvate's effectiveness. But, as with any compound, pyruvate's effectiveness for weight loss is maximized with some type of dietary control.

 Is pyruvate a substitute for reducing calories or increasing exercise?

Pyruvate will help promote fat loss and weight loss on its own. It will help overcome the adverse effects of breaking your diet or exercise program, minimizing the weight gain and fat gain associated with the occasional overeating binge or extra dessert, even for those lucky individuals who are generally able to maintain an "ideal" body weight. However, the effects of pyruvate are maximized with a diet and exercise program, and the effect of whatever diet plan and/or exercise program you engage in will be maximized with the addition of pyruvate. I do not recommend that you use pyruvate as a substitute for reducing calories or exercising. Use them together! You'll be happier with the results.

Pyruvate should not be considered a miracle cure, or cure-all. Your weight goals are very important in determining your weight control program. If all you want is to maintain your weight (which should be a major goal), little dietary restriction of your eating habits, if any, is necessary with pyruvate. However, if you want to lose 80 pounds, a low-calorie diet, along with pyruvate and an exercise program, is a far better approach.

? *Were there enough patients in your studies to support your claims?*

Yes. The effects of pyruvate on body fat and weight in many species—humans, lean and obese rodents, and swine—would suggest these effects to be genuine and consistent. Almost no supplements have been evaluated this extensively. The fact that different scientists, at different universities, at different times of the year, working under different conditions and using different models, all came to the same conclusions about the effects of pyruvate would suggest that pyruvate is legitimate with respect to its effects on fat loss, weight loss, and weight gain.

? *My mother is seventy-one years old and 30 pounds overweight. Would it be beneficial for her to lose weight?*

In a recent editorial in the *American Journal of Clinical Nutrition*, Walter Willet, one of the world's leading academic clinical nutritionists, concludes that moderate weight loss and increased exercise would benefit the quality of life and longevity of the elderly (1997). I agree.

? *My friend has taken pyruvate supplements and says her appetite decreases. Is pyruvate also an appetite suppressant?*

Maybe, but it will take a long time before we'll know with any certainty. As you will see in chapter 9, some consumers report a decrease in appetite and an inability to finish meals while taking pyruvate. I continue to monitor select consumers with questionnaires and personal interviews. However, I have not actually performed controlled, in-depth studies evaluating the effects of pyruvate on appetite.

As my research on pyruvate continues, should our outpatient, anecdotal monitoring continue to suggest that pyruvate decreases appetite, I certainly will investigate this phenomenon. In the meantime, if pyruvate does decrease appetite for at least some of its users, good. A decreased appetite, and subsequent inability to finish meals, certainly would be a help in controlling body weight and fat. In addition, since pyruvate is always circulating in your blood and is always in your heart, liver, and brain tissue; it shouldn't have the adverse effect on heart function that has been recently identified with other appetite suppressants.

? *I have seen, and heard about, some heavy (and not so heavy) people getting fantastic results from pyruvate in control of their weight. I am 5 feet 2 inches tall and weigh 280 pounds. I took pyruvate for two weeks, and it did not seem to help me that much. Why?*

Let's consider the potential reasons why pyruvate didn't work as well as you expected it would.

1. *Dosage.* The effective dose of pyruvate, for most, begins at 3 grams per day and maximizes at 5 grams per day. At your weight, with your goals, 4 to 5 grams per day is the minimum dose you should take. Also be aware that pyruvate is mostly sold in 500-milligram tablets (two tablets = 1 gram), so you need eight to ten tablets per day (two to three with each breakfast, lunch, and dinner) to achieve the proper dose. Remembering to take tablets three times a day is easier said than done. I suggest setting out your daily dose every morning as a reminder. Soon pyruvate nutritional bars, drinks, gums, candies, and cookies will be available, which should help people ingest a sufficient amount of pyruvate.

2. *Quality of the product.* Once the scientific studies and data on pyruvate began to leak into the general press, the expected occurred: There was a great demand for pyruvate. As unfortunately occurs in free enterprise, many unlicensed infringers—producers and distributors with poor quality control—made and sold pyruvate products with little regard for efficacy or safety. As I will discuss in chapter 10, "RTS Pyruvate," we have discovered that many of the first pyruvate products on

the market (not produced by us) contained little, and certainly an ineffective dosage of, pyruvate. If you consumed these ineffective products, you would not benefit much, if at all. We're doing our best to expose and eliminate these ineffective infringer products.

3. *Duration of therapy.* The duration of your therapy (just two weeks) is insufficient to induce a dramatic difference in your weight status. Yes, you would see some effect as a result of pyruvate ingestions within about thirty-six hours, but what would that effect be?

    Even if you were locked in a room and completely starved, with no food and just water, you might lose 5 or 6 pounds the first week (mostly water weight) and maybe 3 to 4 pounds the second week. On an average, mildly restricted weight reduction diet, you might lose 4 to 5 pounds in two weeks. If you barely restricted your diet and didn't exercise, you'd lose even less.

    You should keep the following perspective. Assume, because our data say so, that pyruvate improves fat loss and weight loss a maximum of 50 percent. You are strictly following a 1000-calorie-per-day restricted diet, and without pyruvate you lose 4 to 5 pounds in two weeks. With pyruvate that loss might increase to as much as 6 to 8 pounds. Is that good? Yes! You would see an increased weight loss and no side effects by using a natural compound; and after a month you would weigh 4 to 8 pounds less than you would have without pyruvate. But it would be very difficult to accomplish this in a short time, no matter what you do or take. The recommended rate of weight loss is only 1 to 2 pounds per week. The general belief is that much more weight loss can be dangerous. Pyruvate might increase that safety net to 2 to 3 pounds per week, but that's all. This reasonable amount of increased weight loss assures me that pyruvate ingestion is safe. If pyruvate induced a weight loss of, say, 8 to 10 pounds per week, I would have suspicions about its being toxic and dangerous. Weight loss and fat loss must be slow and consistent over a long time to be helpful in the control of obesity. Pyruvate can make that loss greater, quicker, and more consistent.

4. *Caloric intake.* It is possible that you didn't control your caloric intake and "out-ate" the effects of pyruvate, just as you can out-eat the effects of any weight control agent. As I've discussed, pyruvate "saves" you about 400 to 500 calories per day, or 1 pound per week, or 2 pounds in the best-case scenario. I have encountered some patients who told me they weren't succeeding on pyruvate, only to learn they were eating an extra double cheeseburger (500 to 600 calories per day) while taking pyruvate, and still expected to lose large amounts of weight. It is doubtful that would happen. However, thanks to the weight gain inhibition caused by pyruvate, at least these particular patients didn't gain weight due to the extra calories!

5. *Laws of life.* If you look at the actual numbers in my studies (all of which are listed in the References), you will see that 80 to 90 percent of all humans and animals lost fat and weight on pyruvate, some more than others. To answer your question, you could have been one of the 10 percent of people who didn't get great results while using pyruvate. There are certain unfortunate laws of life and science. Not all supplements and/or pharmaceuticals work the same way for every patient. Remember that the intensity of benefits from any compound varies from patient to patient.

 To summarize, if you weigh 280 pounds and would like to weigh 180 pounds, give yourself at least a year or two to lose the weight, with or without pyruvate supplementation. It would be quicker with pyruvate, by possibly one-third to one-half the time, but you must expect to restrict calorie intake. Please understand your goals as related to normal physiology. Large amounts of weight cannot be lost in a short time. Dietary control and exercise are major armaments for weight reduction, and pyruvate will increase the efficiency of dietary control and exercise, increasing your fat loss and weight loss. Once you achieve your desired weight, since weight control is difficult, it has to be a lifelong endeavor. Pyruvate can help you here, too, slowing fat and weight regain by about 400 to 500 calories per day.

? *My friend told me she was following a 1000-calorie-per-day diet and exercising daily at the gym. She still gained quite a bit of weight.*

It is physiologically impossible for anyone to follow a 1000-calorie-per-day diet, exercise daily, and experience significant weight gain, unless that person is suffering from fluid (water) retention caused by heart, liver, or kidney failure. If this really happened to your friend, she should see her physician immediately. It is, however, more likely that she is not being honest with you. The most plausible explanation for the whole scenario is that she did not follow the 1000-calorie diet and did not exercise to any extent. She may also have underestimated her starting weight.

Obesity is caused by many factors: lack of exercise, decreased metabolic rate, decreased burning of fat, a high-fat diet, and genetics. In general, massive weight gain is rarely associated with massive overeating, contrary to what many have thought. However, none of these factors, except for short-term massive overeating with lack of exercise, can explain a significant, short-term weight gain.

Can pyruvate help your friend? Yes. But to lose a lot of weight requires dietary control and a concerted exercise program. Pyruvate will increase the amount of fat and weight she can lose on the weight reduction diet and will increase her exercise capabilities (discussed in chapter 3). Judging from your friend's recent history with dietary restrictions, however, she will need to make a concerted effort with her diet. A quick fix for obesity is a fantasy. Pyruvate is probably one of the greatest things to come along in a long time for those wishing to lose fat and weight, but it should not be considered a fantasy therapy. It is our new ally against fat gain and weight gain, overweight, and obesity. Let's work with pyruvate to maximize its benefit.

? *Your data suggest that pyruvate has a greater effect on body fat than on body weight. Could I lose body fat without losing much weight? Could it have a sculpting effect on my body?*

Yes. There seems to be little doubt that pyruvate decreases fat formation and enhances fat burning. Even in our human study in which we overfed patients and forced them to gain weight, those patients taking pyruvate had decreased fat deposition. If you are normal weight, or slightly overweight, and consume enough food to meet or slightly exceed your energy needs, pyruvate would decrease your body fat; but since your caloric intake was a little high, your weight would not decrease that much. Your muscle mass might increase, especially if you exercised. Indeed, in our animal body composition studies, those fed pyruvate showed increases in body protein percentage, while body fat percentage decreased, a phenomenon which would meet a definition of a *sculpting* effect. As you will see in chapter 9, normal-weight subjects under no dietary control with no set exercise program still lost noticeable amounts of fat in their thighs and abdomen, with only minimal weight loss. Those subjects with no dietary restriction and low to normal weight at the outset still decreased body fat with pyruvate supplementation.

A recent, double-blind controlled study, performed by New Visions (a licensed pyruvate distributor), scientifically verifies the above. Among the slightly overweight subjects (10 to 15 pounds overweight) on a 2000-calorie diet, which is considered to be a weight maintenance or weight-gaining protocol, who followed a detailed exercise program, those subjects who were taking pyruvate did not lose that much more body weight than those on placebo. However, those taking pyruvate lost almost 5 pounds more of body fat than those on placebo, while gaining 3.5 pounds of fat-free (muscle and water) mass. Pyruvate would seem to be the ideal sculpting agent.

Pyruvate is an ideal fat loss agent, specifically decreasing body fat without decreasing muscle mass. Many of us who are normal weight, who simply cannot exercise that much, or who occasionally overeat during those unavoidable business or social dinners can rejoice that pyruvate causes the human body to resist fat gain due to mild overeating or underexercising.

[?] *I read your human studies on the Internet and found that you used very high doses of pyruvate, sometimes 40 to 50 grams. You recommend 3 to 5 grams as being effective. Why did you use such high doses in these human studies?*

My initial human trials evaluating the effect of pyruvate on weight control were done with dosages 10 to 20 times above the levels I knew were effective. As mentioned previously, initial human trials were part of phase 2, FDA-monitored, clinical trials. In these trials, not only was I evaluating the effectiveness of pyruvate for fat and weight control (which I knew would occur at dosages 10 to 20 times smaller), but also I was investigating, through extensive in-hospital monitoring, whether such high dosages might induce toxicity. They did not.

[?] *I heard an advertisement on the radio that said pyruvate will cause fat loss and weight loss without dieting and exercising. In your previous discussions you stress that a reduced-calorie diet, as well as exercise, should be combined with pyruvate supplementation. Why?*

Pyruvate alone will cause significant fat loss and weight loss without any dietary restriction. (This is evidenced by the soon-to-be-published New Visions study of slightly overweight individuals.) You simply will lose *more* fat and weight by consuming pyruvate in combination with dietary restriction and exercise. This increases your chances of successful, long-term weight control; in addition, you reap the metabolic benefits of dietary restriction and exercise.

? *I am a pet owner. My cat is literally a "fat cat." Will pyruvate help me with the weight control of my pet?*

Yes. The data concerning the beneficial effects of pyruvate on body fat control in many different animal species are overwhelming. Pet food products containing pyruvate for weight control will be available for your pet.

CHAPTER 2

Secret Weapon Against Free Radicals

One of the most exciting discoveries about pyruvate is its ability to scavenge and stop the production of free radicals. To fully understand the significance of this discovery, you need to understand what free radicals are and how they affect you.

Free radicals is a term that's probably familiar to you. You may have recently read an article linking free radicals to heart attacks, or heard a talk show discussion during which experts hypothesized that free radicals contribute to the development of cancer and other diseases. Familiarity, however, is not the same thing as understanding. Because you're constantly bombarded with new information and terminology, it may still be unclear exactly what a free radical is and what it does.

What Is a Free Radical?

Humans must take in oxygen constantly to survive: In this chemical process, oxygen, along with the food we eat, is turned into energy. During this positive conversion, an intermediate and undesirable product is created. This product is an unstable oxygen molecule (O^-), or free radical, as opposed to O_2. While the other, properly processed oxygen molecules go on to serve your body, the unstable free radical molecules head out to create havoc. Most free radicals don't work to build up your body; they work to break it down. Like most radicals, they can attack anywhere.

So why are most of us healthy despite the daily production of free radicals? Because the body, with uncanny knowledge, naturally produces free radical neutralizers.

Antioxidants: The Free Radical Scavenger

Antioxidant is yet another term that may be familiar to you. Commercials exhort consumers to take antioxidant supplements to safeguard against disease; dietitians lecture on the importance of antioxidants, touting them as one more reason to eat a balanced diet. You've gotten the message that you need antioxidants, but do you know exactly what they are? Essentially, *antioxidants* is the populist, all-encompassing term for those entities your body uses to rid itself of free radicals. Acting as scavengers, antioxidants essentially try to "gobble up" the free radicals before they escape into your system. Antioxidants exist in the body at all times. Many are vitamins, which explains why some vitamin supplements are now labeled *antioxidant.* Pyruvate is an antioxidant.

In a healthy person, antioxidants consume most of the free radicals created every day, and most of the remaining free radicals are apparently handled by our systems without causing any visible damage. However, when free radical production increases or the body's scavenging ability is reduced, the excess radicals roaming about the body can start to do damage and can do it very quickly. Free radicals have been associated with everything from heart disease and inflammatory diseases (such as infections, rheumatoid arthritis, and lupus), to DNA breakdown possibly leading to cancer. If free radicals are associated with a multitude of diseases, it stands to reason that control of these free radicals might reverse certain diseases and, even better, prevent disease.

Now that we know this, commercials for antioxidant supplements start to make sense. How better to make sure free radical production doesn't get out of hand than to guarantee we've always got plenty of antioxidant scavengers on hand to fight them? Unfortunately, it's not that simple. Once an oxygen molecule has become unstable, it becomes the very definition of that word. It goes where it wants, it attacks where it wants, and getting it in check is not as easy as you'd hope. Also, the fact that there is no visible free radical damage does not mean that the body is 100 percent normal. Cancer and heart disease, for example, do not develop overnight.

Closing the Barn Door After the Horse Has Gotten Out

As promising as they sound, the many clinical trials using antioxidants for the prevention of disease have been, at best, only promising. Certain antioxidant supplements have not been shown, so far, to either arrest or reverse certain diseases. In fact, the much touted antioxidant beta carotene might even make certain diseases worse (The Alpha-Tocopherol Beta Carotene Cancer Prevention Study Group 1994)! In a study of male smokers (performed in Finland, in conjunction with the National Cancer Institute of the United States), those subjects taking beta carotene actually showed an increase in the incidence of lung cancer (Figure 2.1), while vitamin E had no beneficial effect at all on the incidence of lung cancer (Figure 2.2).

Although this may seem to be a direct contradiction to my earlier assertion of a disease prevention link between free radicals and antioxidants, it isn't. It is simply evidence that the way in which antioxidants eradicate free radicals—and that eradication's relationship to controlling or preventing disease—is far more complicated than we currently understand.

There are numerous hypotheses as to why certain antioxidant treatments have yet to bring free radical production in check. It is possible that specific antioxidants are needed to neutralize specific free radicals, and we may unknowingly send the wrong ones. (For

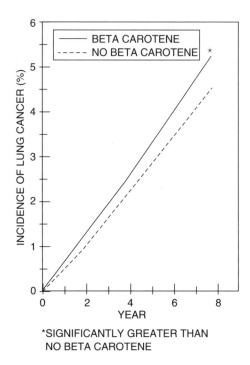

Figure 2.1. *Lung cancer incidence in subjects with and without beta carotene supplement.*

Source: The Alpha-Tocopherol Beta Carotene Cancer Prevention Study Group, "The effect of vitamin E and beta carotene on the incidence of lung cancer and other cancers in male smokers," *The New England Journal of Medicine* 330 (1994): 1029–35.

example, a patient may be taking massive amounts of vitamin C, when vitamin E is the antioxidant that's really needed to combat the particular problem.) Certainly some antioxidants are far more effective than others. The Cambridge Heart Antioxidant Study suggests that known heart disease patients taking 800 international units of vitamin E (25 times the presently recommended dose) for at least two years showed a 30 to 60 percent reduction in major cardiovascular events (Stephens et al. 1996).

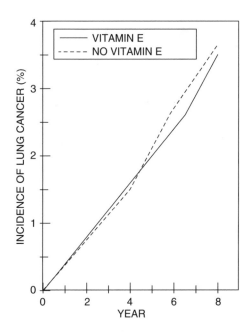

Figure 2.2. *Lung cancer incidence in subjects with and without vitamin E supplementation.*

Source: The Alpha-Tocopherol Beta Carotene Cancer Prevention Study Group, "The effect of vitamin E and beta carotene on the incidence of lung cancer and other cancers in male smokers," *The New England Journal of Medicine* 330 (1994): 1029–35.

It may be that, to make a difference, antioxidant supplement dosage levels should be far higher than those administered in the latest research, or that current dosage levels need to be administered for a longer time.

However, it is most likely that the real problem with attempting to utilize antioxidants to bring free radical production in check is that we are trying to control something already out of control; in other words, we are closing the barn door after the horse has gotten out. This brings us to the benefits of pyruvate in combating free radicals. Studies have shown that pyruvate is a scavenger that can attack, and eliminate, free radicals once they've been produced (Salahudeen, Clark, and Nath 1991), but pyruvate also does something far more important: Pyruvate supplements sharply reduce the production of free radicals, and it is the only nontoxic compound until now identified to do so!

Preventive Medicine Against Free Radicals

As the saying goes, an ounce of prevention is worth a pound of cure. As the following studies make clear, I can definitively link pyruvate supplementation to the prevention of free radical formation.

There is something else about these studies of note, before I go on. As they occurred well into the research on pyruvate, after it became clear that pyruvate could be a marketable product, it was important that the research be conducted without the possibility of manipulation or impropriety. So although I designed the research, I did not execute most of it. This research was done in a *double-blind study*. One team was given solutions labeled *A* and *B* and told how to use them, without knowing what they were. A second team analyzed the findings, also under *A* and *B* labels. Not until I received the blind study data did anyone know what pyruvate was able to do. Indeed, the research teams performing the studies had little idea that pyruvate was involved at all. We did a number of carefully controlled studies to validate that pyruvate did indeed prevent free radical production.

Study Number 1: Making Magic with Solitary Cells

For the first study, we started with the smallest and most controllable entity—an isolated cell. We removed cells from a rodent, and we bathed some cells in a pyruvate solution and other cells in a placebo. We then cut off all the oxygen to the cells, leaving them in what researchers call an *anoxic* state. Two things happen when a cell is rendered anoxic. First, free radical production stops, because clearly you can't produce renegade oxygen molecules if you don't have any oxygen. Second, the cell eventually dies.

Having stopped all free radical production, we reoxygenated the cells to see what effect, if any, pyruvate would have on the newly revived cells and on subsequent production of free oxygen radicals as oxygen became available to the cell.

In the placebo cells, the reaction was exactly what we expected. The cells were dying, and free radical production had gone wild. In the pyruvate cells, however, the results were astonishing. Not only was free radical production at a minimum, but also there was little cellular death (Figures 2.3 and 2.4) (Borle and Stanko 1996).

We Can Help an Animal's Cell, But Can We Help the Animal?

Now that I knew we could alter free radical production and cellular death in a carefully controlled environment, it was time to try the theory on a living creature.

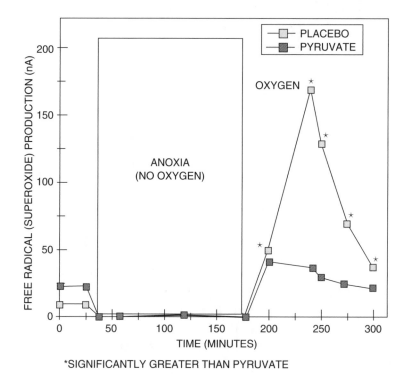

*SIGNIFICANTLY GREATER THAN PYRUVATE

Figure 2.3. *Free radical production in isolated liver cells.*

Source: A. B. Borle and R. T. Stanko, "Pyruvate reduces anoxic injury and free radical formation in perfused rat hepatocytes," *American Journal of Physiology* 270 (1996): G535–40.

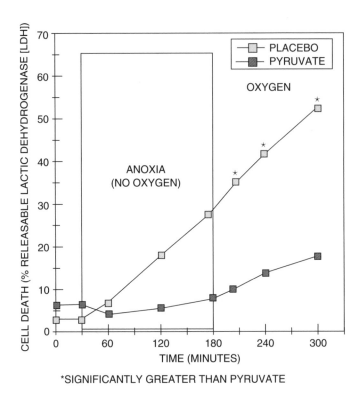

Figure 2.4. *Cell death in isolated liver cells.*

Source: A. B. Borle and R. T. Stanko, "Pyruvate reduces anoxic injury and free radical formation in perfused rat hepatocytes," *American Journal of Physiology* 270 (1996): G535–40.

In the second study, we injected pyruvate into the intestines of one group of animals and a placebo into the second group. After the rendering of anoxia or ischemia and then reoxygenating, analyses of these tissues showed more good news. Once again, there was massive cell death and, with a supply of oxygen, massive free radical production in the ischemic animals treated with placebo. However, cells in the animals treated with pyruvate were 90 percent normal (Figure 2.5) (Cicalese, Lee, Schraut, Watkins, and Stanko 1996).

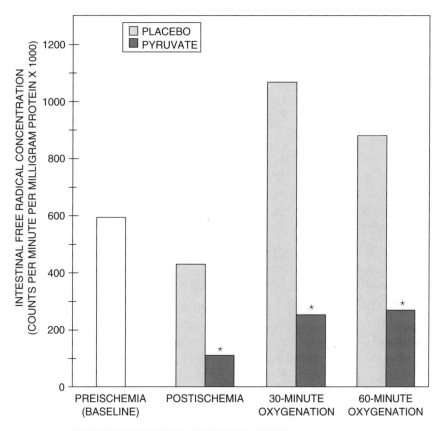

Figure 2.5. *Free radical concentration in intestine.*

Source: L. Cicalese, K. Lee, W. Schraut, S. Watkins, and R. T. Stanko, "Pyruvate prevents ischemia-reperfusion mucosal injury of small rat intestine," *American Journal of Surgery* 171 (1996): 97–101.

Antioxidant Champ?

In the third study, it was time to determine the benefits of ingesting pyruvate supplements, rather than concentrating pyruvate in a specific organ.

To do this, I now used three groups of rodents and gave all a drug called *Clofibrate*. Clofibrate has been shown to successfully lower blood cholesterol, but unfortunately it can have negative side effects. One of the common side effects in rodents is liver disease, a condition directly linked to increased free radical production.

The diet of the first group was supplemented only with Clofibrate, the second group with Clofibrate taken in conjunction with the antioxidant vitamin E, and the third group with Clofibrate and pyruvate. At the end of the feeding period, the rodent livers were analyzed.

The animals who were given only Clofibrate showed an expected increase in liver size (40 percent) and weight (75 percent). Vitamin E did not diminish these unfortunate side effects. Pyruvate, however, reduced them by 70 percent (Stanko et al. 1995). Pyruvate had actually prevented what's known as *morphologic* damage, or that damage which is visible to the naked eye. (For instance, a healthy lung's pink color is its normal morphologic state; a blackened lung is one which has suffered morphologic damage.) This pattern continued with free radical production. Pyruvate prevented free radical production; vitamin E did not (Figure 2.6). However, as expected, both vitamin E and pyruvate scavenged free radicals equally (Figure 2.7). Overall, pyruvate actually prevented the damaging free radical production, and organ disease, associated with ingesting Clofibrate.

In summary, our studies indicate that in isolated cells, organs, and with general supplementation, pyruvate stopped the production of free radicals, scavenged free radicals, and prevented cell death.

Fighting Free Radicals in Two Ways

Now that I've demonstrated pyruvate's ability to prevent the formation of free radicals, and the subsequent damage they can do, I will go into a little greater detail about how and where pyruvate attacks on the free radical chain.

When free radicals form, a chain reaction of disaster occurs that creates several stages of damaging free radicals, each stage capable of causing more harm than the one before. The first free radical formed is called *superoxide*. If you prevent it from forming,

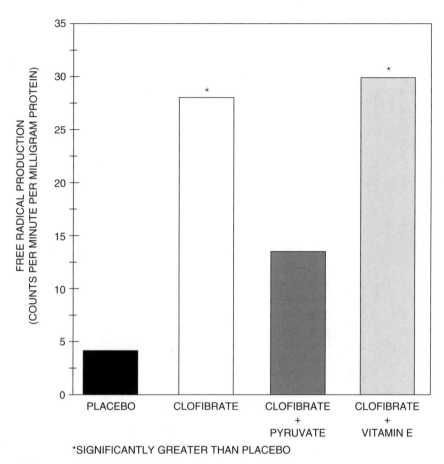

Figure 2.6. *Free radical production in liver.*

Source: R. T. Stanko, G. Sekas, I. A. Isaacson, M. R. Clarke, T. R. Billiar, and H. S. Paul, "Pyruvate inhibits Clofibrate-induced hepatic peroxisomal proliferation and free radical production in rats," *Metabolism* 44 (1995): 166–71.

you'll prevent the formation of the free radicals it spawns. This is exactly what pyruvate does. It stops the production of the super-oxide free radical and consequently all the free radicals that would follow (Figure 2.3).

If the superoxide free radical does form, it quickly breaks down into a series of deadly radicals which get increasingly hard to contain (Figure 2.8).

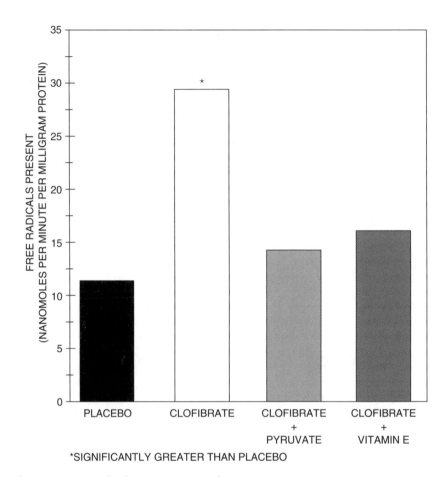

Figure 2.7. *Free radical concentration in liver.*

Source: R. T. Stanko, G. Sekas, I. A. Isaacson, M. R. Clarke, T. R. Billiar, and H. S. Paul, "Pyruvate inhibits Clofibrate-induced hepatic peroxisomal proliferation and free radical production in rats," *Metabolism* 44 (1995): 166–71.

SUPEROXIDE ⟶ HYDROGEN PEROXIDE ⟶ HYDROXYL ION (OH⁻)

Figure 2.8. *Breakdown of the superoxide free radical.*

The hydroxyl ion is a bad one!

Pyruvate also scavenges farther down the free radical chain; it eliminates hydrogen peroxide and therefore the hydroxyl ion. Consequently, pyruvate can help prevent the production of free radicals and help to bring the problem under control once free radicals have gotten out of hand. Pyruvate would seem to be terrific at controlling free radicals, but it doesn't go overboard and wipe them all out. This is important because, believe it or not, as harmful as too many free radicals may be, it seems the human body needs some of them.

Free Radicals: Often the Cause, But Sometimes the Cure

In spite of all the harm they can cause, free radicals do some good as well. When you develop a bacterial infection such as pneumonia, the body sends white cells to combat the disease. These white cells then go on to release both enzymes and free radicals that attack the bacteria and defeat the disease. If pyruvate destroyed all the free radicals, this could interfere with the body's normal functioning. Somehow (I don't know exactly how), pyruvate manages to get rid of damaging free radicals but leaves behind the free radicals we might need.

Since we have free radicals in our system at all times, it seems reasonable to assume that even if they're not causing serious disease, they may be consistently causing some small degree of damage at all times. That damage may well contribute to what we accept as the most normal of human conditions—aging.

Free Radicals: Contributors to the Aging Process?

We all age, but clearly some do it better than others. Free radical production could be part of the reason why.

Hypothetically, let's say that the free radicals we carry around chip away a little bit at a time at our systems. It is known that they're linked to arthritis, heart disease, and the maladies associated with aging. They may well also contribute to our gradual slowing down. Smokers can certainly attest that the increased free radical production that results from smoking affects not only internal health but also external appearance. For instance, smoking frequently shows up in the quality and texture of the skin.

Why do some people look great at age fifty while others look every bit their age and maybe more? Well, barring plastic surgery and expensive health and beauty treatments, a youthful fifty-year-old may naturally, and through diet or supplement, be doing a far better job of minimizing free radical production. By diminishing the formation of free radicals and slowing cellular death, pyruvate may well slow what we accept as the natural process of aging.

Now, what I'm talking about here can mean living longer but also, more important, living better. By slowing or stopping the manifestation of disease, adding pyruvate to our diets may well help level the genetic playing field, giving us the good health and energy that we envy in our more youthful-seeming peers.

Can I say with certainty that there will be such across-the-board benefits from pyruvate? No. Not only would definitive studies be difficult to control because of the numbers of people and decades of tracking involved, but also all of us involved in the current research about pyruvate will have gone to heaven before such a study could be completed. However, my many research trials (along with anecdotal evidence and common sense) suggest that pyruvate could make a difference when it comes to preventing the problems associated with free radicals. Since too many free radicals manifest as signs of aging, it stands to reason that diminishing free radical production might reduce some of the problems we currently view as the inevitable by-products of growing older. I recommend a recent review published in the medical journal *Science* entitled "Oxidative stress, caloric restriction and aging" (Sohal and Weindruch 1996) for those readers interested in further explanations that are beyond the scope of this book.

My studies lead me to believe that we don't have to accept chronic pain, hugely diminished physical capabilities, and low energy as automatic components of aging. The more research I do, the more I think that looking and feeling good at age seventy isn't simply a matter of luck but is something we can all reasonably strive for. How we age and our ability to enjoy life are things over which we should be able to exert some control.

How we age isn't the only thing that seems to be passed down from one generation to the next. Forms of cancer and heart disease are some of the conditions linked to free radical production that have long been considered to "run in the family." However, with pyruvate's potential for prevention, these diseases may no longer have to be viewed as inevitable parts of our lives.

More About Pyruvate and Prevention

Nothing is more exciting to me than pyruvate's prospective role in the prevention of disease. Certainly, it is exciting to contemplate the potential for using other antioxidants to successfully scavenge free radicals and treat their related diseases. But why treat a problem if we can prevent it? And I think that's pyruvate's proven effect on free radicals.

I certainly know that pyruvate can't hurt. It exists in our bodies and in our food, and in no instance during any of my trials on either humans or animals have I found that pyruvate opened the doors to disease, or indeed had any side effects at all. The potential benefits, however, are enormous.

Preventing disease is good not only for the individual who would otherwise be suffering but also for the families who want more time with ailing relatives. Preventing disease is good for consumers who reap the benefits of decreased disease and decreased medical costs. Ask any family who would give anything for another basketball game with Dad or an afternoon tea with a favorite sister. The possibility of improving not only the length, but also the quality, of life is one they would grab in a minute.

Pyruvate might also help prevent symptoms in somebody already stricken with disease. For instance, continued excessive free radical production can contribute to the symptoms and suffering of patients stricken by such inflammatory diseases as lupus and rheumatoid arthritis. Cut the production, possibly cut symptoms, possibly cut the pain, and a patient has the potential for a whole new lease on life.

There is one more thing. Some of the potential help that pyruvate might offer in diminishing the symptoms of illness may already be available through ingesting a pharmaceutical drug. However, unlike most drugs, pyruvate doesn't seem to have side effects, and there is no worry about deleterious interaction with other medications. While some medications may cure one symptom but create another, pyruvate does not seem to contribute to a breakdown in the body's ability to function.

I am not implying that pyruvate should replace already effective medications, but it might supplement such therapies, offering new benefits and/or enhancing therapies.

So, when it comes to free radicals, pyruvate prevents and protects; it scavenges without going overboard and interfering with the body's normal functioning.

To illuminate the potential scope of benefits associated with pyruvate's inhibition of free radical formation, I offer the following list of diseases or conditions identified in the *Annals of Internal Medicine* (Cross et al. 1987) as being associated with excess free radical production:

1. Inflammatory immune injury, including vasculitis and autoimmune disease
2. Ischemia, anoxia, reoxygenation states
3. Drug- and toxin-induced reactions
4. Iron overload
5. Nutritional deficiencies
6. Alcoholism
7. Radiation injury
8. Aging
9. Cancer
10. Amyloid disease
11. Lead poisoning
12. Malaria
13. Sickle-cell disease
14. Anemia
15. Lung disease, including cigarette smoking, emphysema, pollutants, acute respiratory distress syndrome, and bronchopulmonary dysplasia
16. Heart disease
17. Atherosclerosis

18. Kidney disease
19. Rejection of transplant organs
20. Liver disease
21. Rheumatoid arthritis
22. Parkinsonism
23. Senile dementia
24. Hypertensive cerebrovascular injury
25. Cerebral trauma
26. Demyelinating disease of the brain
27. Cataracts
28. Degenerative retinal damage
29. Retinopathy
30. Contact dermatitis
31. Sun injury to skin (Cross et al. 1987)

Q & A: Free Radicals

? *If antioxidants such as vitamins E and C are proven free radical scavengers, why haven't they yet tested successfully in the treatment of disease?*

The problem probably lies not only with the antioxidants themselves but also with our continued ignorance of exactly how to use them. We may be asking vitamin C to do a job that only vitamin E can do. With pyruvate, this might not be a consideration. We don't have to figure out how best to attack free radicals with pyruvate around—it has already stopped them from forming! The difference between pyruvate and other antioxidants is that the other antioxidants come into play once a free radical has been formed, while pyruvate actually stops the free radical from forming at all (as well as scavenges it once it's shown up).

? *You've discussed pyruvate's effectiveness in dealing with cellular death in intestinal organs. Would it be effective in preventing cellular death within the brain as well?*

The answer is yes. It seems that most cells that are sick, diseased, and dying produce excess free radicals, and that process of forming free radicals is the same in all cells. The symptoms are different: Free radicals in your brain may cause you to become comatose, while those in your knee cause the less traumatic arthritis and its resulting pain. Pyruvate has also been shown to be helpful in preventing nerve cell death.

? *A lot of the benefits of pyruvate described in this book are backed up with some very impressive research. Your statements about pyruvate and aging, however, seem to me to push the edge of the envelope. Am I wrong?*

No, you're not wrong. Unfortunately, I'll never do a study on aging, because I'm too old. Despite chronic doses of pyruvate, by the time the results are in, I'll be researching the next life. In all seriousness, studies on aging in the laboratory cannot be compared to studying actual aging in people. However, all the evidence on pyruvate and free radical production would suggest that pyruvate is beneficial in the aging process. Also, as far as I am aware, pyruvate is the only natural, nontoxic compound that has been shown to prevent free radical production. So why not take it? Studies are being initiated. I hope you take pyruvate so you can live long enough, and well enough, to hear the results.

? *As all your research has been on animals, and you've done no long-term, double blind clinical trials on humans, why do you think pyruvate will work when some of the other antioxidants have not been proved to do so?*

My belief in pyruvate's potential is far from simply speculative. First, I have performed trials on intact, living animals. Prior to clinical trials, other antioxidants were tested mainly on isolated organs. Vitamin E is one antioxidant that's been proven to be effective in certain disease trials, while pyruvate has been proven more effective in comparison trials. Also, remember, pyruvate enters the cell far more freely than other antioxidants, which is another indicator of potential for superior antioxidant performance. It's not expensive, it's not toxic, and I would certainly rather use it now than find out ten years from now that it could have made a big difference in my life, but I didn't give it a chance. I'll say it again: Pyruvate prevents free radical production, and no other antioxidant does. I am absolutely, scientifically convinced of pyruvate's potential benefit in the control of free radicals.

CHAPTER 3

Improving Exercise Capability

As the U.S. public has become more aware of the benefits of exercise, a lot of dietary supplements have come on the market promising the exercise enthusiast improved performance and greater stamina. "Use this," the promoters seem to suggest, "and you'll lift more weights, run more miles, and feel better while you do it." Some of you may have tried these products and have seen little measurable improvement in your performance. I bring this up for an important reason: I'm about to tell exercise enthusiasts (and those of you who haven't been too enthusiastic) that by taking pyruvate you will have improved performance, greater stamina, and, yes, you'll feel better while you are exercising. But why believe me? Because I've got the research to back it up! I have data, more data, and most important, reproducible data.

If my claims sound too good to be true, I understand. Until I started this research and collected the data, I couldn't have agreed with you more. My data have passed the scrutinizing eyes of my peer physicians and scientists and are published in the most prestigious medical journals. If the data hadn't been published, I wouldn't be writing this book about it.

With Pyruvate, One Thing Leads to Another

Once again, my studies on pyruvate and exercise started because of the findings of another study, the study on liver fat content that inspired my research into pyruvate's effect on weight control.

When I analyzed the contents of the rodent liver during that earlier research, I found both decreased fat content and increased glycogen (glucose) content. This is significant because at the time the scientific community had come to a generally shared conclusion that the body's primary fuel for exercise was glycogen (stored glucose). Although muscle glycogen is considered the primary fuel source for exercise, I hypothesized that glycogen in the liver might fuel it as well and that increased glycogen (an increase in glucose fuel) might increase exercise capability in animals and humans alike.

Tomorrow's Doctors, Today's Laboratory Subjects!

For this research, I shifted to clinical trials on human subjects done in conjunction with the Health and Physical Education Department, the Human Energy Laboratory, and the Clinical Research Center at the University of Pittsburgh.

For these two studies, the first of which was done in 1986, I looked at a group of male dental and medical students. They were in good shape, fit and healthy, but in no way extraordinary, trained physical specimens.

We had no hope of keeping a dozen or so males in their early twenties in the research center for the weeks before the study. Our subjects were paid. We controlled their diet; the students ate most meals at the center. They agreed not to ingest any alcohol or drugs or to deviate from the diet in any way (we were able to successfully monitor this).

To account for individual variables, we did what is known as a *crossover study*. Group A was given pyruvate with food for a week before the first round of tests; group B was given a placebo. The tests were conducted, after which the students took two weeks off, allowing their systems to normalize. The next time, group A was given a placebo and group B the pyruvate supplement. In this way, with each subject testing once with pyruvate and once with a placebo, the difference in each individual's performance could be accurately charted, and individual personal variables, while not eliminated (being present during both the placebo and pyruvate evaluations), did not affect the study's accuracy.

We must offer a word of appreciation to our subjects. In order to perform the most accurate study possible, we put our subjects through some very uncomfortable procedures, including putting a catheter into their arteries, a process so exacting we had to bring a surgeon in to do it.

There was purpose to our seemingly unkind methods. We wanted to measure the subjects' metabolite turnover during, before, and after vigorous exercise. *Metabolites* refer to anything that is biochemically produced during normal function and during physiologic study. Metabolites vary with activity—we produce different amounts of metabolites when we're exercising than we do when resting.

Most studies only measure the metabolites in *venous blood*, that is, the blood that is carried away from the muscle by the vein, which shows the by-product of exercise. But that does not tell you what was actually used or made by the muscle during exercise. To find that out, we needed to measure the metabolites as they came into the muscle via the arteries, and out of the muscle in the venous blood, during exercise.

So we set up subjects for the first tests, which involved arm exercise (Stanko, Robertson, Spina, Reilly, Greenawalt, and Goss 1990). The exercise machine we used is commonly employed by heart patients—the arms work in the same sort of pedaling motion as feet on a bicycle—and it does a phenomenal job of stimulating the heart. Subjects were monitored by four exercise physiologists.

The subjects were pushed to exercise until they simply could not exercise any more. They were egged on by coaches with scripted encouragement: Each coach used exactly the same language so that one coach could not push subjects harder than another coach. The subjects breathed through an oxygen tube and communicated how they were feeling during the exercise by pointing at a chart posted on the wall in front of them, numbered from 1 (feeling great) to 10 (exhausted).

The first noted effect was that the subjects on pyruvate seemed to be exercising with greater ease than the subjects on placebo (they'd point to 4 when the placebo subjects pointed to 6). Next, we found that the pyruvate subjects were able to exercise an average of 20 percent longer than the placebo subjects (Stanko, Robertson, Spina, Reilly, Greenawalt, and Goss 1990). Not only did they exercise longer, but also they exercised much more efficiently until they finally "hit the wall" and stopped. They didn't get tired and slowly wind down, as most of us do during exercise. They exercised at near-maximum capacity until they came to an abrupt stop. But remember: They had exercised an average of 20 percent longer.

To clarify, here is an example of how pyruvate might make a difference during a regular gym workout. Say you normally do twelve bicep curls with 15 pounds, but by curl eleven you are really starting to lose form, fighting to do those last two reps. With pyruvate, however, you might do sixteen bicep curls, the last of which would be done with nearly the ease as the first. However, after that sixteenth curl, you find you cannot do one more rep, that a final push is not a consideration. However, since you have already exceeded your usual rep capacity, the ability to do that final push is certainly not missed!

Now we go back to the study. The subjects were exercising longer, with greater ease and efficiency. Why? To find out, we analyzed the metabolic results.

We did a muscle biopsy. The level of glycogen in the arm muscle wasn't that much greater in the pyruvate group than in the placebo group. These data could not completely explain why the pyruvate subjects seemed to do so much better at exercise.

Then we analyzed glucose uptake in the muscle, and this is where we found exciting results. In the pyruvate group, the muscle had a far more efficient uptake of glucose, which is the fuel for exercise. Whereas it might normally take up a glucose content of

10, say, it now had an uptake of 20 (Figure 3.1). This finding could easily explain the increased exercise capability of the pyruvate subjects.

As I've said, glycogen (stored glucose) is the major fuel for muscle activity. Now, as anyone who's been in a car knows, the more fuel there is, or the more efficiently the engine can use this fuel, the farther the car can go. In the pyruvate subjects, the muscle was actually able to utilize more of the glucose fuel available in the blood supply than that in placebo subjects. It's as if there existed a substance to put into the gas tank to enable the engine to run 150 miles (more efficiently) on a full tank of gas, whereas previously it had only been able to run 120 miles because, thanks to the supplement, the car engine could make more efficient use of the gas. How does pyruvate do this? It is possible that liver glycogen or insulin action influenced the fuel supply to the muscle.

So improved glucose uptake seems to explain the ability to exercise longer, but it doesn't necessarily explain the change in exercise efficiency. In other words, even if you could do sixteen reps instead of twelve, why weren't reps fifteen and sixteen as difficult as reps eleven and twelve had previously been? Why were the subjects exercising to such a full capacity before stopping, instead of slowly tiring out as they normally did?

I have no proven answer, but I do have a hypothesis.

Exercise and Free Radicals

The scientific and medical communities agree that most of the conditions every human being experiences—aging, exhaustion, and so forth—are caused not by one thing but by a combination of them. Exhaustion is a perfect case in point.

Because glucose is accepted as exercise "fuel," depletion of glucose or glycogen is certainly accepted as an element of muscle exhaustion. It is not, however, believed to be the only cause. Our exhausted subjects still had glucose in their blood. Muscle exhaustion might also be linked to increased free radical production during exercise (Kanter 1995).

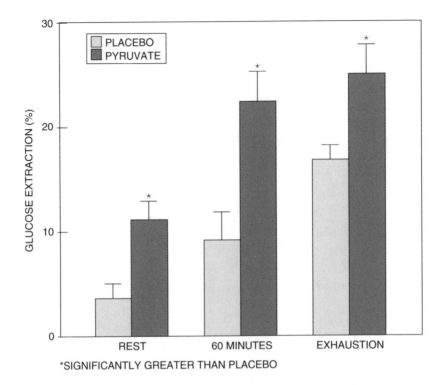

Figure 3.1. Arm glucose extraction in subjects performing arm exercise.

Source: R. T. Stanko, R. J. Robertson, R. J. Spina, J. J. Reilly, Jr., K. D. Greenawalt, and F. L. Goss, "Enhancement of arm exercise endurance capacity with dihydroxyacetone and pyruvate," Journal of Applied Physiology 68 (1990): 119–24.

They're Baaaaaack

When you exercise, free radical production greatly increases. Many exercise physiologists feel that this production contributes to exhaustion, or gradual slowing down, during exercise.

We already know that pyruvate greatly reduces free radical production. So if free radicals are what cause the slowing, and pyruvate has eliminated many of them, then our subjects' new exercise capability makes a great deal of sense.

Why then do they stop, or "hit the wall"? Why didn't pyruvate turn our "average" subjects into superathletes? A car can be made more efficient, but it can't be turned into a Ferrari. You might be able to run 8 miles with pyruvate supplementation, instead of your normal 6 miles (some of our subjects actually improved exercise endurance by 50 percent), but you will not run 42 miles. There are numerous scientific theories as to why a person becomes exhausted and simply can't continue exercising, some sooner than others. Eventually everybody tires, even an Olympic athlete.

We Did It Once. Can We Do It Again?

I took our findings to a conference on exercise. Most scientists were excited by what looked like a promising study; but it was, in truth, only one study. The question was, Could I duplicate my somewhat spectacular findings?

A year after I conducted my first study, I did a second. We recruited a new group of students and put them through the exact same drill. When it came to test day, this time we placed catheters in their legs and then exercised their legs. This was quite a procedure because, compared to the arm, we were dealing with an enormous muscle, and the catheters had to be placed in the subjects' groin areas.

To my surprise and delight, our results were exactly the same. The subjects' leg exercise capability, muscle glucose uptake, and sense of well-being during exercise were improved with pyruvate in a nearly identical fashion to the first group's arm exercise a year before (Table 3.1 and Figure 3.2) (Stanko, Robertson, Goss, Spina, Reilly, and Greenawalt 1990). I wouldn't have believed it if I hadn't seen it myself. Remember, this was a double-blind controlled study that I designed, but it was performed and scrutinized by other independent, doubting scientists.

Feeling Groovy

I've mentioned that the subjects felt better during exercise, and now seems a good time to discuss that. As I've said, there was a chart on the wall (Figure 3.3) for the subjects to point at, to indicate how they were feeling during exercise. Note that, at the outset, I thought this chart had little scientific value. How could something as subjective

Table 3.1. Endurance Capacity During Prolonged Leg Exercise

Subject No.	Endurance Time after Placebo Diet (Minutes)	Endurance Time after Pyruvate Diet (Minutes)
1	60	76
2	70	80
3	52	78
4	77	85
5	62	67
6	60	80
7	61	83
8	84	80
Total	66± 4	79 ± 2*

*Significantly greater than placebo.

Source: R. T. Stanko, R. J. Robertson, F. L. Goss, R. J. Spina, J. J. Reilly, Jr., and K. D. Greenawalt, "Enhanced leg exercise endurance with a high-carbohydrate diet and dihydroxyacetone and pyruvate," *Journal of Applied Physiology* 69 (1990): 1651–56.

as feelings be included in a scientific study? Wouldn't the subject's feeling of well-being during exercise have as much to do with whether he was having a bad day, or had received glowing praise from a professor, as it would with his actual physiologic condition? Even the presence of a psychologist to help monitor the subject's moods did little to sway me regarding the potential accuracy of this portion of the study. (Data that are good, sound, and reproducible are the only data that I'll sign my name to.)

Every subject who took pyruvate showed a marked psychological improvement during exercise compared to what he felt during the same test when taking the placebo (see Figure 3.4) (Robertson et al. 1990). This was true no matter what the subject's initial mood. The data proved to me that I had to believe it. Of course, as we've already shown, no matter what the mood, pyruvate consistently enhanced physical performance.

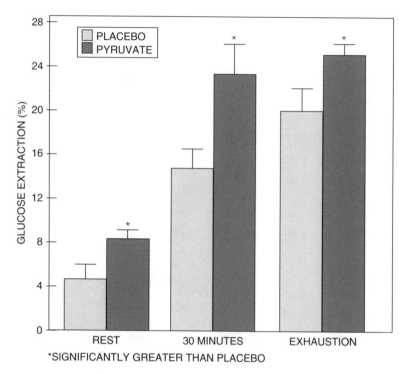

Figure 3.2. *Leg glucose extraction in subjects performing leg exercise.*

Source: R. T. Stanko, R. J. Robertson, F. L. Goss, R. J. Spina, J. J. Reilly, Jr., and K. D. Greenawalt, "Enhanced leg exercise endurance with a high-carbohydrate diet and dihydroxyacetone and pyruvate," *Journal of Applied Physiology* 69 (1990): 1651–56.

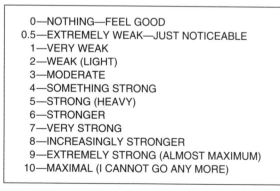

Figure 3.3. *Ratings of perceived exertion.*

Heart-Smart with Pyruvate

Yet another surprising piece of information was uncovered when I analyzed the data on the exercise subjects. Although the subjects were working a lot harder, their hearts weren't. Yes, their heart rates were increased, but not nearly to the levels expected given the increased duration of their exercise performance. This led me

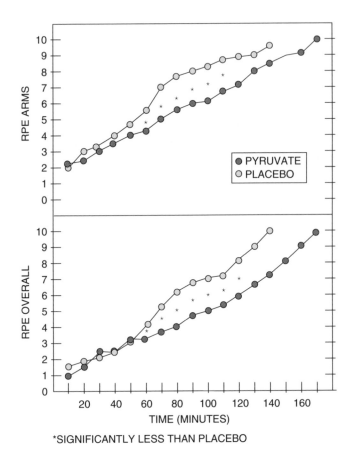

*SIGNIFICANTLY LESS THAN PLACEBO

Figure 3.4. *Rating of perceived exertion (RPE) on arms and total body in subjects performing arm exercise.*

Source: R. J. Robertson, R. T. Stanko, F. L. Goss, R. J. Spina, J. J. Reilly, Jr., and K. D. Greenawalt, "Blood glucose extraction as a mediator of perceived exertion during prolonged exercise," *European Journal of Applied Physiology* 61 (1990): 100–5.

to wonder if pyruvate was affecting cardiac output or the heart's ability to pump blood. Of course, I did a study and identified (in the anesthetized dog model) that pyruvate increases heart pumping ability and efficiency. I discuss this study in detail in chapter 4.

Q & A: Pyruvate and Exercise

[?] *Pyruvate seems to improve the performance of the average person. Would it do the same thing for a superathlete?*

There should be some improvement, but it's hard to imagine that a superathlete could jump 50 percent higher or run 50 percent farther (as some of our subjects did) than he or she does right now. However, it could give slight improvement or help pick up the slack during times that the superathlete is overtired or recovering from an injury or an illness. I would love to do a study on it, but elite athletes have such rigid lifestyles, diets, and schedules that they can't follow the specific protocol necessary to do accurate trials. I certainly hope they'll give pyruvate a try and would be interested to know if they find it makes a difference. *Note:* Athlete Shannon Miller trained with pyruvate supplements prior to winning a gold medal in the 1996 Atlanta Olympic Games. She said she could train harder and longer. She did not take pyruvate during competition.

[?] *Do you think pyruvate will be approved for use by Olympic athletes during competition?*

Hopefully. Although pyruvate supplementation increases the natural body levels by approximately 5 to 10 times, it is a natural supplement, and it's always found within the body (heart, brain, liver, etc.). Since pyruvate has no side effects and is found in our bodies and our diets at all times, it should be considered an enhancing, rather than a doping, agent.

| ? | *You've tested pyruvate on men. What about exercise benefits for women? Are they the same?*

There's no physiologic reason to think the benefits would differ between men and women. The processes of glucose uptake in the muscle and free radical inhibition are the same in women and men. Many anecdotal reports and preliminary trials identify that pyruvate is as helpful to women as to men. Ask Shannon Miller about her successes with pyruvate.

| ? | *You've studied a small group of men under somewhat idealized conditions. Do you have any evidence that pyruvate works for exercisers outside the laboratory?*

As a matter of fact, I do. Preliminary trials and many anecdotal reports identify an improved capacity for exercise in the untrained, "normal" population consuming pyruvate. One of my attorneys, for instance, runs the hillside steps in Santa Monica, California. With pyruvate, he went from being able to run them eight times to being able to run them twelve times. Others report increased weight-lifting ability, longer runs, and more sit-ups. These anecdotal findings accurately reflect what we learned in the laboratory.

CHAPTER 4

Heart: Energy, Efficiency, and Protection from Ischemia

As members of an advanced, industrialized society, we most fear cardiovascular disease, primarily heart disease. There is no question that atherosclerosis and subsequent cardiac ischemia (lack of oxygen) begin to develop in a person's early twenties; and heart disease, the result of long-term ischemia, is a major cause of death. Free radical production is a primary culprit in the induction of ischemic cardiac disease.

As my research progressed into the 1980s, more and more preliminary evidence suggested that pyruvate might have some benefit for the heart. At the same time, other researchers were identifying benefits for the heart provided by pyruvate. Consequently, in studies evaluating other effects of pyruvate, I began to investigate the effects of pyruvate on the cardiovascular system.

In studies evaluating the effects of pyruvate on exercise endurance, heart rate did not increase to the same extent as did exercise capacity (Stanko, Robertson, Goss, Spina, Reilly, and Greenawalt 1990). This finding suggested increased cardiac efficiency with pyruvate supplementation. In obese subjects consuming a high-fat diet who were being evaluated for the effects of pyruvate on cholesterol metabolism, cardiac efficiency (the ability to pump blood without utilizing large amounts of oxygen) was increased with pyruvate supplementation (Stanko et al. 1992).

Having seen these results, I and others began to very intensely investigate the effects of pyruvate on cardiac function in many animal models and in human studies. The results of these studies are the subject of this chapter, and I feel certain that you'll find them as exciting as I did.

Energize

As I mentioned in chapter 3, pyruvate supplementation increases exercise capacity by as much as 50 percent. It does so mainly by increasing the efficiency with which muscles, such as the leg and arm, extract fuel or energy (glucose) from the blood. Even as I deciphered the data revealing the finding that pyruvate indeed increased fuel supply to large muscles, I wondered whether pyruvate might have a similar effect on heart muscle. Heart muscle is a totally different muscle from arm or leg muscle, and the heart utilizes a different fuel mixture to function than other muscles do. As I designed a protocol to evaluate the effect of pyruvate on heart energy stores and utilization, I was pleasantly surprised to find that some of the work had already been completed by Rolf Bunger, M.D., Ph.D., at the Uniformed Services Medical School in Bethesda, Maryland. Dr. Bunger, a physiologist, measured different heart cellular metabolites as an indicator of heart energy or *phosphorylation* potential. These types of studies are tedious and exacting, and to explain them would be even more tedious and exacting. So I won't. I will simply summarize the results.

In varying conditions, such as normal pumping of blood (*baseline functioning*), the stress of increased heart rate, and pathologic conditions similar to the classic heart attack secondary to ischemia, pyruvate perfusion of the heart increased cellular energy from 50 to 200 percent (Bunger, Mallet, and Hartman 1989; Mallet and Bunger 1993)! These studies have been repeated and verified, and there seems little doubt that pyruvate increases cellular energy even at rest, without the demands of exercise.

Dr. Bunger's data showing that pyruvate increased energy stores before there is even a demand for that energy (baseline) corroborated my findings in exercising subjects who showed increased muscle fuel (glucose) extraction at baseline, even before the stress of exercise (Figures 3.1 and 3.3).

As you will read in chapter 9, many subjects who consume pyruvate report feelings of increased energy to perform everyday activities. The fact that pyruvate can enhance the body's energy state is not a hypothesis or an exaggerated claim—it is backed up by irrefutable, reproducible data showing increased cellular uptake of fuel energy (glucose) and increased cellular energy content (phosphorylation potential) with pyruvate supplementation.

Efficiency

There is no doubt that pyruvate increases cellular energy, especially in the heart. The question is, Exactly what does that mean in terms of heart function? As I was reviewing the aforementioned studies, I decided to do a study to look at what effects (if any) on heart function could be seen with pyruvate perfusion.

It's a Dog's Life

In brief, we evaluated heart function in dogs as we infused pyruvate. We measured cardiac output (the amount of blood the heart pumps out), the amount of pressure that the heart produces to pump blood, and the oxygen utilization during this entire process (Yanos, Patti, and Stanko 1994). As we infused pyruvate to higher and higher concentrations (2 to 5 millimoles in the blood), we did indeed find that pyruvate had beneficial effects on heart function. Cardiac output increased by 50 percent (Figure 4.1), the pumping pressure of the heart increased by 50 percent (Figure 4.2), and not so surprisingly, the oxygen utilized in this increased work done by the heart was far less than expected (Figure 4.3).

The reason I say *not so surprisingly* is that Dr. Bunger, in ongoing studies done on isolated heart cells, also showed that pyruvate increased cardiac work without increasing the amount of oxygen

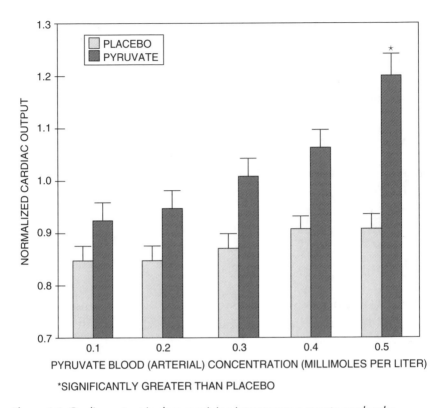

Figure 4.1. *Cardiac output in dogs receiving intravenous pyruvate or placebo.*

Source: J. Yanos, M. J. Patti, and R. T. Stanko, "Hemodynamic effects of intravenous pyruvate in the intact, anesthetized dog," *Critical Care Medicine* 22 (1994): 844–50.

required. This is a very important finding. Here's why. There are many, many drugs in use today in cardiac care units that will increase both cardiac output and the pumping pressure of the heart to a much greater extent than the use of pyruvate alone can—both good things for someone with a diseased heart. However, these inotropic drugs (drugs used to improve cardiac pumping ability) also increase the amount of oxygen necessary to fuel the heart's pumping ability. Why is this an issue?

Here's the problem. If you have a sick heart, most likely it is because you don't get enough oxygen to the heart muscle. You're in a bind: You need to increase your heart's ability to pump because, since you are sick, it's not pumping blood and oxygen

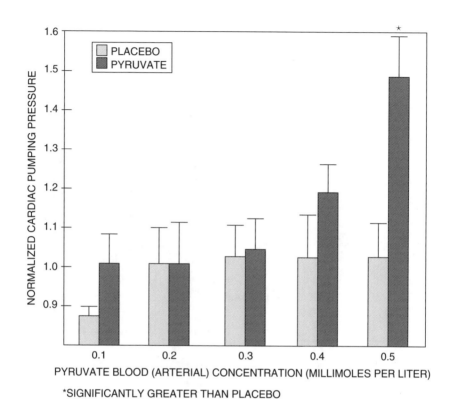

Figure 4.2. *Cardiac pumping pressure change in dogs receiving intravenous pyruvate or placebo.*

Source: J. Yanos, M. J. Patti, and R. T. Stanko, "Hemodynamic effects of intravenous pyruvate in the intact, anesthetized dog," *Critical Care Medicine* 22 (1994): 844–50.

properly. However, the heart is not functioning properly as a result of not having received enough oxygen to produce energy and work. Consequently, many cardiac drugs, while good for you, are self-limiting because they require increased oxygen use for their efficacy—oxygen which is already deficient to begin with. Pyruvate, however, would not seem to be in this same category and, indeed, would seem to be an ideal inotrope because it increases pumping pressure but does so without increasing the need for oxygen that much.

This is important even if you're not in crisis in the cardiac care unit. The truth is, if you're forty to fifty years old, there's a good possibility you have some degree of atherosclerosis, a condition

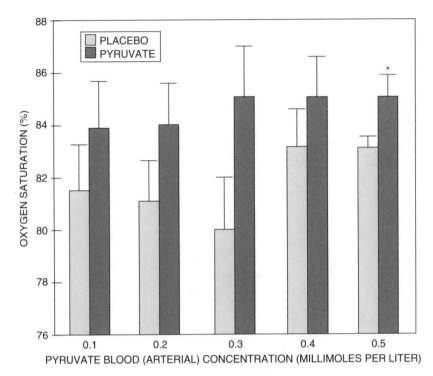

*SIGNIFICANTLY GREATER THAN PLACEBO
†GREATER OXYGEN SATURATION IN VENOUS BLOOD INDICATES LESS
OXYGEN UTILIZED FOR HEART FUNCTIONING.

Figure 4.3. *Venous oxygen saturation in dogs receiving intravenous pyruvate or placebo.*[†]

Source: J. Yanos, M. J. Patti, and R. T. Stanko, "Hemodynamic effects of intravenous pyruvate in the intact, anesthetized dog," *Critical Care Medicine* 22 (1994): 844–50.

that decreases daily the amount of oxygen available for the heart to use in pumping. The less oxygen, the less cardiac pumping. The less cardiac pumping, the less blood to heart vessels, further worsening the already deficient oxygen supply to the heart. Sometimes this condition progresses to the point where your heart can't perform enough work, and you experience the classic heart failure and/or heart attack. Pyruvate should enable the heart to pump more blood for the given amount of oxygen present, even if it's deficient, and should benefit those who have early, but not debilitating, atherosclerosis and/or heart disease. If you have debilitat-

ing heart disease, pyruvate will still benefit you, but you will probably also require additional drugs for best results. Actually, pyruvate might make certain cardiac drugs more efficient and
beneficial.

Protection

You might rightly be questioning whether I ought to be extrapolating results from a healthy dog regarding an unhealthy condition. I
didn't do this in a vacuum, though. I had the luxury of access to
the additional knowledge and findings of my colleagues, who
were simultaneously evaluating the effects of pyruvate in animal
models of heart disease. Most used different models and different
experimental conditions of heart disease. Nevertheless, all revealed
identical (and very exciting) benefits of pyruvate for the heart.

To begin, I'll go to my colleague Dr. Rolf Bunger in Bethesda,
Maryland. Dr. Bunger evaluated the effects of pyruvate in the
ischemia-reperfusion model of heart disease. To quickly review,
this model reflects what happens to the human heart with chronic
ischemia, such as seen before and during heart attack. Now a little
about ischemia, so we can better understand the magnitude of the
findings of these studies.

Ischemia is the state in which an organ is unable to function at
its best because it's receiving inadequate blood constituents, such
as all-important oxygen. This can happen because of an actual
decrease in blood constituents or because, even though the blood is
normal, the ability to get it to the organ is decreased. The most classic example is seen in patients with coronary artery disease and
atherosclerosis. Their blood vessels are no longer normal because
they're clotted with plaques and platelets; so no matter how good
the content of the blood, it simply can't get where it needs to go.
The heart then becomes oxygen-deprived and is unable to properly
function, further worsening the blood supply to the heart itself.
This ischemic state also shows up in conditions involving other
organs such as the brain and/or small intestine. A narrow and/or
clotted carotid (neck) artery, a condition particularly common in

older people, keeps blood and oxygen from the brain, rendering the brain ischemic and, in the worst scenario, resulting in a stroke.

Heart-Smart!

If you're reading this and you're in your twenties or thirties, you may be thinking that heart disease is a long way off. In truth, damage to the heart starts a lot earlier than is believed. Doctors who examined young soldiers in Vietnam were stunned to discover how many were showing early signs of atherosclerosis at the ages of twenty-three or twenty-four years. If you're a smoker, this may be even truer for you. Evidence which supports this concern is summarized in an editorial in *The New England Journal of Medicine* by J. M. Gaziano, entitled "When Should Heart Disease Prevention Begin?"(1998).

My initial belief that pyruvate could be helpful in the treatment of ischemia goes back (as so many of my studies have) to the findings on pyruvate and free radicals. Most doctors believe that the damage from an ischemic condition is incurred because ischemia results in the overproduction of free radicals.

Ischemia: A Free Radical Rampage

To understand the cause and effect of ischemia and free radical production, first imagine your heart. For a moment, the blood supply is decreased or cut off; your heart is rendered ischemic. Now, in that moment, not many free radicals are being produced because free radicals come from oxygen, and at that point your heart isn't getting enough oxygen. Next, blood supply is returned (reperfusion), and your heart is reoxygenated, or else you die. At that point, free radical production escalates, and the free radicals are off on their usual rampage—in this case damaging and killing heart cells. Ironically, the event you hope for—getting blood flow back to the major organ, thus enabling your survival—is doing a lot of damage, even while it's maintaining your life! Time and again, in one cardiac study after another, this free radical overproduction has been shown to be the major culprit in ischemic damage.

This is how using antioxidants to minimize the risk of heart disease became a popular idea. An in-depth review of this concept, "Antioxidants and Atherosclerotic Heart Disease" by F. H. Epstein, M.D., appeared in *The New England Journal of Medicine* (1997). But these antioxidant scavengers, with the exception of vitamin E, have yet to be proved particularly effective. Besides, controlling free radicals isn't easy. You're a lot better off simply keeping them from showing up.

In the above scenario, you have a period of ischemia; but luckily, for whatever reason, your heart becomes reperfused and you are alive. You will find, though, depending on the severity of the disease, that your heart may not be able to pump blood with the same pressure and blood flow (cardiac output) that it did before the incident, because the muscle is now damaged. For you to continue to survive, your heart must pump enough blood (despite being sick) to your other vital organs and itself. Therefore, the goal of all cardiac rehabilitation (beginning immediately after heart damage and continuing thereafter) is to maintain adequate heart pumping pressure and cardiac output, maintaining enough oxygen to enable the heart and other vital organs, such as the brain, to work.

Now we go back to Dr. Bunger's ischemia-reperfusion studies and the benefits of pyruvate in diseased hearts. Dr. Bunger measured heart pumping pressure developed by sick, reperfused hearts that were simultaneously perfused with pyruvate (Bunger, Mallet, and Hartman 1989). As seen in Figure 4.4, the pressure produced with pyruvate perfusion was far greater than that without (placebo). Concurring with our studies of the normal heart, Dr. Bunger also saw an increase in pressure produced by the diseased heart with increasing concentrations of pyruvate (Figure 4.5). He did not, however, find any benefit of other metabolites such as lactate, acetate, or glucose (Bunger, Mallet, and Hartman 1989).

Over There

In another interesting study, this time done quite a distance from my Pittsburgh base, Italian investigators evaluated the effects of pyruvate supplementation prior to inducing heart attack in animal

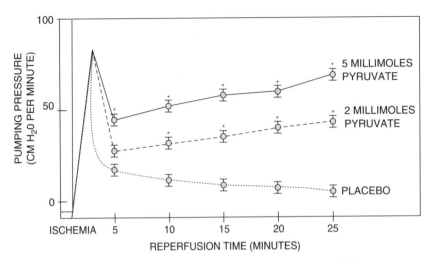

*STATISTICALLY GREATER THAN PLACEBO (GLUCOSE + LACTATE)

Figure 4.4. *Cardiac pumping pressure with reperfusion after ischemia.*

Source: R. Bunger, R. T. Mallet, and D. A. Hartman, "Pyruvate-enhanced phosphorylation potential and inotropism in normoxic and postischemic working heart," *European Journal of Biochemistry* 180 (1989): 221–33.

models. Heart attack was induced in the same fashion as in Dr. Bunger's studies (Cavallini, Valente, and Rigobello 1990). Because the Italian investigators perfused pyruvate before and after ischemia-reperfusion injury, it mimics the effects of subjects pretreated with pyruvate prior to suffering severe heart damage.

Pyruvate enhanced the pressure produced by a severely damaged heart (Figure 4.6). Cardiac energy subsequent to severe damage was also improved with pyruvate supplementation. There was no benefit derived from other metabolites such as lactate, acetate, or glucose.

Here We Go Again!

In a study done at the University of Nebraska Medical School by Lawrence Deboer, M.D. (Deboer et al. 1993), rodents were evaluated for cardiac pressure and mechanical function after ischemic

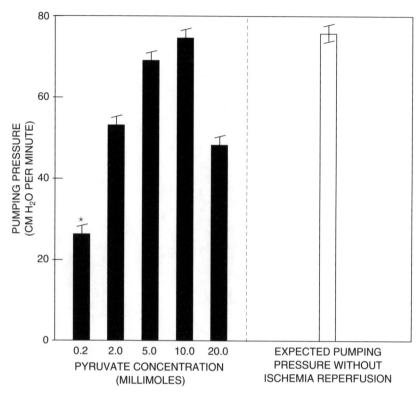

*SIGNIFICANTLY SMALLER THAN EXPECTED WITHOUT
ISCHEMIA-REPERFUSION INJURY

Figure 4.5. Cardiac pumping pressure with different concentrations of pyruvate after twenty-five-minute reperfusion subsequent to ischemia.

Source: R. Bunger, R. T. Mallet, and D. A. Hartman, "Pyruvate-enhanced phosphorylation potential and inotropism in normoxic and postischemic isolated working heart," *European Journal of Biochemistry* 180 (1989): 221–33.

damage and reperfusion. In addition, they were monitored for free radical production, which we've already established increases dramatically during reperfusion and reoxidation of an ischemic organ. Dr. Deboer's focus was on whether there was a correlation between the recovery of the heart and prevention of free radical production.

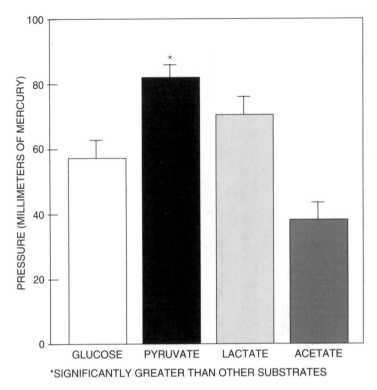

Figure 4.6. *Heart pumping pressure generated after ischemia and reperfusion with different substrates.*

Source: L. Cavallini, M. Valente, and M. P. Rigobello, "The protective action of pyruvate on recovery of ischemic rat heart: Comparison with other oxidizable substrate," *Journal of Molecular and Cellular Cardiology* 22 (1990): 143–54.

Life in the Midwest

Because I, and Dr. Bunger, had identified that the most effective dosage of pyruvate for the protection of the heart was from 2 to 5 millimoles in the blood or in perfusate, Dr. Deboer chose to use the lowest effective dose of 2 millimoles of pyruvate in his studies (extrapolation to oral supplementation would be approximately 2 grams per day). Even with this relatively low dosage of pyruvate (which is still 5 to 10 times that usually found in a normal cell), heart-pumping pressure produced subsequent to heart damage (Figure 4.7) and mechanical function of damaged hearts (Figure 4.8)

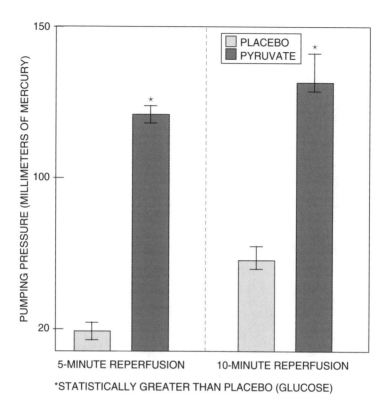

*STATISTICALLY GREATER THAN PLACEBO (GLUCOSE)

Figure 4.7. *Heart pumping pressure with reperfusion after ischemia.*

Source: L. W. V. Deboer, V. A. Bekx, L. Han, and L. Steinke, "Pyruvate enhances recovery of rat hearts after ischemia and reperfusion by preventing free radical formation," *American Journal of Physiology* 265 (1993): H1571–76.

were improved with pyruvate supplementation. As more evidence for the free radical theory of cardiac damage with reperfusion, Dr. Deboer showed that while pyruvate was enhancing the pressure generation capacity of the heart, it was also dramatically decreasing free radical production (Figure 4.8).

So it certainly would seem that excessive free radical production is involved in cardiac damage with heart attack. Without a doubt, pyruvate will prevent this excessive free radical production and enhance the pumping capacity of the heart after ischemia, reperfusion, and heart attack damage.

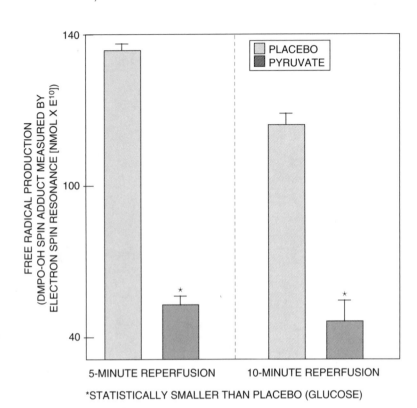

Figure 4.8. *Free radical production with reperfusion after ischemia.*

Source: L. W. V. Deboer, V. A. Bekx, L. Han, and L. Steinke, "Pyruvate enhances recovery of rat hearts after ischemia and reperfusion by preventing free radical formation," *American Journal of Physiology* 265 (1993): H1571–76.

The Human Element

What about human studies? These were all animal studies. Because they were repeatedly reproduced and were done by different scientific investigators at various scientific institutions, it would take an extreme skeptic (scientist or not) to doubt the validity of these findings and their potential for human benefit. Cardiac studies are very difficult to do in a human population for obvious reasons, but these studies are under way, and results have already been presented at National Cardiology Scientific presentations.

Dr. Gerd Hasenfuss of the University of Freiberg, Germany, evaluated the effect of infusing pyruvate into the coronary artery of human subjects suffering from congestive heart failure. These patients have damaged hearts that cannot pump blood adequately. The blood sits in their lungs, resulting in "congestion," inadequate oxygen uptake, and severe shortness of breath. This is not an uncommon sequela to heart attack. The human subjects infused with pyruvate showed improvement in the ability of their diseased hearts to pump blood, decreased lung congestion, and improved cardiac energetics. At the time of this book's publication, these exciting data had only been presented to the scientific community at conferences.

This study is very similar to one I initiated, in which I gave ambulatory patients with congestive heart failure 4 to 5 grams of pyruvate daily and evaluated their ability to exercise. Many people with congestive heart failure have very little exercise capacity because their diseased hearts cannot pump enough blood or oxygen to the exercising muscle or to the heart itself, and the subsequently congested lungs cannot utilize breathed oxygen. This study was designed to be a crossover study: The same subject received pyruvate for three weeks and exercised; then repeated the study, receiving placebo for three weeks, and exercised; and the results were compared (the same type of study was referred to with healthy medical students in chapter 3). The initial results are very exciting. Two out of three subjects exercised much longer and with minimal shortness of breath (severe shortness of breath would be expected during exercise with their cardiac condition). However, this study is not complete, and further evaluation is necessary before conclusions can be drawn.

So What Do I Have to Say . . .

All the above studies and data convince me that the nontoxic, natural metabolite pyruvate is of monumental benefit to the heart, whether it is preventive or used in those patients with cardiac damage.

Free Radicals in Animals

As I mentioned previously, ischemia reperfusion injury occurs in organs other than the heart. Being compulsive, and always questioning the veracity of any generated data, I wanted to know if the dramatic effects of pyruvate on free radicals and ischemia-reperfusion injury in the heart were specific for the heart or would occur in other organs also. As you might have guessed, I did a study.

We fed, and then perfused, the intestines of animals with pyruvate or placebo, caused ischemia, and then reoxygenated. In the placebo-treated animals, free radical production greatly increased, and the small intestine developed damage and cellular death. In those animals treated with pyruvate, free radical production after reoxygenation was greatly reduced, as were small intestine damage and cellular death identified as ischemic injury (Cicalese, Lee, Schraut, Watkins, and Stanko 1996).

So, since ischemia-reperfusion injury and free radical production are similar in different organs, the beneficial effects of pyruvate on these maladies are not specific to the heart and should be similar in different organs.

Q & A: Heart and Energy

[?] *I've had a heart attack and I take a few cardiac medications. I really can't recall them all. It would seem to me that pyruvate could benefit me. Would it interfere with my other medications? If I take it, should I stop taking my other medications?*

It certainly would seem that pyruvate might be ideal for you because of its capacity for increasing cardiac pumping ability without increasing oxygen demands. There is no reason to expect a negative interaction between pyruvate and any other beneficial cardiac medications. I do not, under any circumstances, recommend discontinuing any cardiac medication unless so advised by your physician. In your case, with known heart disease requiring medication, pyruvate should be more of an enhancement than a substitute. However, if you are working on a second heart attack, and you certainly could be, every potential benefit can be a life-saver. The "metabolic" rehabilitation with the natural compound pyruvate would certainly seem to be worth a try.

[?] *At my age (fifty-three), I don't take any cardiac medications, but I am concerned about the presence of atherosclerosis. Would pyruvate be of benefit to me?*

Prevention of coronary artery disease and subsequent heart attack has to be considered one of the major goals of medicine. The fact that pyruvate is a natural compound, circulating in our blood at all times, suggests that supplementation with a higher dose (3 to 5 grams per day) would not have much potential for side effects. Therefore, it might be an ideal preventive agent for you. The over-whelming benefits of pyruvate identified in normal and diseased hearts (atherosclerosislike models) would identify pyruvate as one of the only well-studied natural compounds that might be used for the prevention of heart disease. There is no question that irre-spective of symptoms that might be related to the heart, many of us, even at young ages, are continuously developing the potential for the devastation of heart attack. Therefore, it would seem inju-dicious not to recommend pyruvate as a compound that could benefit you in the fight against this devastating disease. At your age, you are by no means considered an older person, but I, and others, think that pyruvate would even benefit those in their late twenties and early thirties as a preventive agent against the devel-opment of heart disease.

[?] *My doctor told me to take aspirin to thin my blood and prevent platelet clumping (aggregation), which would be beneficial in the prevention of atherosclerosis and eventual ischemic heart disease. Have you found any evidence that pyruvate might inhibit platelet aggregation?*

Yes, I have. As with other ongoing pyruvate studies, at present, these studies are not complete and have yet to be published. In preliminary studies in my laboratory, I find that pyruvate inhibits platelet aggregation seen in blood vessels in the liver subsequent to liver transplantation. I am continuing the evaluation of the effects of pyruvate on platelet clumping (aggregation) and function as well as on other blood coagulation parameters. Still, there would be little reason to believe that platelet function in the liver differs from that in the heart. Would I take pyruvate under the assumption that I'm beneficially affecting platelet aggregation? Absolutely, without a doubt.

? *I'm one of those skeptics. You don't have large, multicentered clinical trials evaluating the efficacy of pyruvate in heart disease. Don't you think we ought to wait until those are complete?*

Some of us can't wait, in particular those of us with heart disease. There is no other nontoxic supplement available with anywhere near the data that back up the efficacy of pyruvate in normal and diseased heart models. As I have stated in other sections of this book, these trials are extremely time-consuming and expensive. I do not say they are not advisable, but such trials are not required for approval of the use of pyruvate. Because pyruvate is nontoxic and is in our diet, blood, heart, and brain, it is reasonable to recommend supplementation at this time.

? *At the risk of sounding naïve, why would I want to increase cellular energy?*

Life is the production of energy. Despite the fact that most of us eat to satisfy our appetites and our taste buds, we actually consume food stuffs to produce energy. Metabolism of any foods eaten results in the functioning of the mitochondria to produce phosphorylated compounds, or energy, which is life. To be able to increase energy, pyruvate supplementation, which is scientifically proven without a doubt (unlike most other claimed "energy-producing" compounds), would seem to be an ideal way to literally enhance your life, as you'll read in chapter 9.

? *You mention studies of energetics done in heart cells. Can you extrapolate this to other cells in the body?*

Because most cells have mitochondria (the energy-producing organelle of your body) and pyruvate functions in the same way in all these mitochondria, it is logical to assume that pyruvate enhances and affects the energetics of more cells than just the heart. Preliminary studies in my laboratory suggest this is so. Verbal reports of subjects who consume pyruvate identify a generalized energetic state that is not usually experienced. It is doubtful that these subjects would experience improved functioning in everyday activities if only heart cells were energized.

? *The studies you mention in this chapter concerning the effects of pyruvate on the heart show benefits with a blood level seen with consumption of 3 to 5 grams per day by mouth. The study from the University of Nebraska found dramatic effects of pyruvate on the heart with only 2 millimoles (2 grams per day). If I'm taking pyruvate as a preventive agent for heart disease, would 2 grams be adequate? What if I have had a heart attack? Would the same dosage apply?*

If you already have had a heart attack and you have a known debilitating heart disease, I would give it my all and take as high a dose as is therapeutically effective, which is 4 to 5 grams per day. Prevention, however, which typically involves many years of treatment, would probably require a lower dosage over a long time. Since most scientific investigators have shown that 2 to 4 millimoles of pyruvate in the human blood system initiates beneficial effects of pyruvate in the heart, it would not be unreasonable to take 3 to 4 grams of pyruvate as a preventive measure with respect to heart disease.

? *I'm in great shape. I run 5 miles per day, watch what I eat, and don't get chest pains or shortness of breath. My doctor says I check out fine. Isn't it a little excessive to suggest that we all need to worry about ischemic heart disease?*

First, my intention is not to get anybody worried. It sounds as if you'll be living a long and healthy life. Still, there is no question that cardiac disease starts at a young age, and coronary arteries do not become clogged overnight. You can have almost severe coronary artery disease without chest pain, not to mention having the earliest manifestations of heart disease without its showing up on any tests. Remember, too, that no matter how healthy, fat-free, and smoke-free our lifestyle, everybody makes free radicals at all times, and free radicals are, without a doubt, linked to an ischemic condition. So, since you're doing so many things right already, why not consider a benign, natural metabolic prevention such as pyruvate to guard against ischemic disease and/or free radical production? If you still think you're invincible, you might want to find out just how many men sixty-nine years old on their second heart attack were once strong and healthy athletes when twenty-five years old. Ask them how much two more years without a heart attack would mean to them. They'll probably do a better job than I ever could of clarifying just how important this prevention can be.

? *Are you saying pyruvate prevents heart attack?*

No, but the data on the beneficial effects of pyruvate on cardiac ischemia are overwhelming. As I have stated, clinical trials of a large group of subjects will be necessary to absolutely, scientifically, without a doubt verify that pyurvate is beneficial to the heart. Even then, the difficulty of maintaining dietary and lifestyle control of such a large group for such a long time would render the results questionable. I'm too old to wait, and since the only thing I have to lose is time spent in cardiac rehabilitation, I'm personally willing to give pyruvate a chance. I hope you will, too.

? *I recently heard that the vitamin folate might be protective in the heart. What's your opinion, and would taking it preclude my taking pyruvate?*

Some studies suggest that cardiac disease is associated with the production of homocysteine. It seems that folate inhibits this increase. Again, since folate is a natural compound, why not take it? As far as taking it along with pyruvate, folate would in no way inhibit pyruvate's effect, and it is highly doubtful that any negative reaction would result from doing so. Hypothetically, they might even complement each other.

? *My father-in-law has periods of disorientation and short-term memory loss, and he occasionally passes out. His doctor informs me this is a result of his having "transient ischemic attacks of the brain." Would pyruvate be helpful for him?*

Yes. Your father-in-law's condition is a result of loss of oxygen to the brain and/or increased free radical production (ischemia-reperfusion injury). Because pyruvate is beneficial for both of these conditions, it should help the brain. From my personal communication with scientists at the University of Washington's School of Medicine in St. Louis, Missouri, evidence is mounting that pyruvate protects against nervous system disease.

? *The information you have presented suggests to me that pyruvate would be beneficial for my dog's cardiovascular system. Am I correct?*

Absolutely correct. For the sake of space and time, I have discussed only a small portion of the voluminous data identifying the beneficial effects of pyruvate on the cardiovascular system of companion animals, such as your dog. Specialized heart products containing pyruvate and other compounds deemed to be beneficial for the heart (similar to the marketed human products) will soon be available for your companion animal.

CHAPTER 5

Diabetes

I discovered pyruvate's potential benefits in the treatment of some types of diabetes in the same way I had discovered many of pyruvate's other benefits: by analyzing the data of an unrelated clinical trial. In this case, my study of pyruvate's enhancement of exercise capability led me to investigate pyruvate's potential for helping Type 2 diabetics.

As discussed in chapter 3, pyruvate increases the muscle's glucose uptake. For this reason, I felt that it might be useful in the treatment of Type 2 diabetes, which is characterized by increased glucose production in the liver and impaired glucose muscle uptake. Why Type 2 diabetes? Before I proceed, it's important to clarify the difference between the two types of diabetes.

When we think of diabetes, many of us think of insulin injections, strictly regimented eating times, and carefully monitored blood sugar levels. This is the treatment for Type 1 diabetes, which typically shows up when the patient is quite young. In Type 1 (insulin-dependent) diabetes, the pancreas shuts down and ceases to produce insulin, making insulin injections necessary. Type 1 is usually far more severe than Type 2 diabetes and, fortunately, less common.

Type 2 diabetes usually occurs far later in life, commonly in patients who are suffering from obesity. This type generally is treated with pills that stimulate the pancreas to produce insulin. Type 2 diabetes is usually accompanied by other symptoms common to obesity, such as heart problems and elevated blood pressure. Unfortunately, Type 2 diabetes is becoming increasingly common, rising with the percentage of obese people in the United States. Subjects with this non–insulin dependent diabetes were utilized in my study.

Even a Little Can Mean a Lot

I evaluated seven obese women with non–insulin dependent (Type 2) diabetes. The women were kept on a 1500-calorie diet for two weeks as outpatients; and they stayed in the research center under our supervision for the third week, during which time some were fed pyruvate supplements along with their meals and others were fed a placebo. The subjects served as their own controls. That is, on one visit they were given pyruvate, on another visit they were given a placebo, and the results were compared (Stanko, Mitrakou, Greenawalt, and Gerich 1990).

When I analyzed the data, I found that patients with elevated blood glucose levels benefited from pyruvate supplementation because their blood glucose levels were reduced by an average of 16 percent. However, ingestion of pyruvate did not lower the glucose levels in those patients whose glucose level was stable and did not render the patient hypoglycemic. Pyruvate acted as a blood glucose stabilizer, in just the same way aspirin works with a fever. If your temperature is high, aspirin will help bring it down to normal. However, if your temperature is normal, aspirin usually will not bring it down any lower.

What does this mean to you? Most diabetes experts feel that even a small improvement and/or control of blood glucose levels would delay the complications that we all fear: infections, kidney disease, and eye disease.

While I was happy about these findings, I certainly couldn't call them conclusive. In fact, these unexpected benefits, along with all the others, seemed too good to be true. However, unbeknownst to me, as I was questioning my exceptional findings, a researcher I'd never met was doing studies that would completely corroborate the results of trials on diabetic patients.

Nearly Blind Mice

At Washington University in St. Louis, Missouri, Joseph Williamson, M.D., was experimenting with the use of pyruvate to treat diabetic eye disease in animals. In this particular study, Dr. Williamson was able to normalize blood flow through the eye and, most important, stop the leakage of a protein called albumin through the blood vessels by actually perfusing the eye with pyruvate solution. This leakage is a serious complication of diabetes, associated with many abnormalities, including decreased vision.

Good News, and More Good News

My research team and others had now confirmed that pyruvate was beneficial in both lowering blood glucose levels and inhibiting some of the severe complications of diabetes. But there are still more benefits, because diabetes rarely exists in a vacuum.

Major risk factors in diabetes are elevated blood pressure, elevated blood cholesterol level, and/or heart disease. I have shown that pyruvate has a mild effect toward reducing blood pressure (Stanko, Reiss Reynolds, Lonchar, and Arch 1992). Pyruvate has also been tested on obese patients with elevated cholesterol levels who eat a high-fat diet. I found that pyruvate mildly inhibits the effect of this high-fat diet on the blood cholesterol level (Stanko, Reiss Reynolds, Lonchar, and Arch 1992). Last, pyruvate has myriad beneficial effects on the normal and diseased heart. Most of these effects are mild, but they're there. For a patient suffering from any combination of these diseases, the possibility of an across-the-board beneficial effect, no matter how minor, is certainly positive.

So This Means . . . ?

Pyruvate, a natural compound, improves blood glucose levels in diabetes, inhibits the complications of diabetes in the eye, and has a positive effect on many of the accompanying diseases of diabetes.

Q & A: Diabetes

? *Pyruvate has a mild effect on the problems associated with diabetes, but there are already medicines available that have been shown to have a similar or even greater effect. Why should I use pyruvate?*

First, pyruvate is a natural supplement with no known side effects. The same cannot be said of the many diabetic medications available, almost all of which have some side effects. Also, as I've discussed, diabetes is frequently accompanied by other diseases which require other drug treatments, so drug interaction becomes an issue. Pyruvate has beneficial effects on all these diseases with no interactions. There are no known reactions from taking pyruvate along with medications, and pyruvate may actually enhance the effectiveness of some medications. I do not, however, recommend stopping your already effective diabetes medication. What I am saying is that there is no reason not to take pyruvate along with these medications.

? *I suffer from hypoglycemia (low blood sugar). If pyruvate is known to lower blood glucose levels, could taking it be a problem for me?*

It seems that pyruvate only lowers blood glucose when it's abnormally high and has no effect when it's normal or low. I don't understand how pyruvate knows when to lower blood glucose levels, and when to leave them alone; I'm just happy that it does. So, no, there should be no ill effects from taking pyruvate for those suffering from hypoglycemia. Actually, in the disease of alcohol-induced hypoglycemia, pyruvate has been suggested as a potential therapy.

? *What about Type 1 (insulin-dependent) diabetes? Have you done trials to see if pyruvate is beneficial in treating it?*

No, I haven't. However, Dr. Williamson's research in successfully treating diabetic eye disease, a common accompaniment to Type 1 diabetes, leads me to believe there may be some benefit for Type 1 diabetics in taking pyruvate supplementation. And, again, because it's natural with no known side effects, it shouldn't hurt and may well help. Anecdotally, one Type 1 diabetic patient reports a 100 milligram per deciliter decrease in blood glucose while taking pyruvate.

? *Some Type 2 diabetics eventually need insulin as their disease worsens. Would pyruvate help prevent the need for insulin?*

I think it would help. Work by John Ivy, Ph.D., at the University of Texas at Austin (Ivy et al. 1994), suggests that one of the benefits of pyruvate is to increase the effectiveness of insulin (insulin sensitivity). So, in Type 2 diabetes, where the body produces an insufficient amount of insulin, pyruvate may increase the effectiveness of whatever insulin is produced, such that you might not need to add to the body's supply through injection.

? *I heard that free radicals might be involved in the deterioration of pancreatic function. You've talked about pyruvate and free radicals, and it seems to be effective against them. Could this be a beneficial effect of pyruvate on diabetes?*

Absolutely. If abnormal free radicals are indeed part of the diabetic process, pyruvate certainly would seem to be beneficial in eliminating these free radicals and inhibiting the onset of the disease and/or the complications which follow. Preliminary but incomplete data in my laboratory would suggest just such an effect.

? *I've read that pancreatic cells are being transplanted into diabetic patients. Would pyruvate be beneficial to that process in any way?*

Again, absolutely. Also again, preliminary data in my laboratory, this time more extensive, would suggest a benefit, and I will talk about it in chapter 7.

? *You mention that pyruvate is beneficial for diabetic eye disease. What about another eye disease—cataracts?*

Many animal studies identify that pyruvate both impedes the formation of cataracts and shrinks cataracts after they are formed. This is all the more reason to believe that pyruvate is an ideal preventive and/or well-being supplement.

CHAPTER **6**

Cancer

I'd be hard-pressed to find a reader of this book whose life hasn't been affected in some way by cancer. Almost everyone knows, or is related to, a person who has suffered from, and in the best circumstances survived, cancer. Even those researchers whose field of study is not primarily cancer are continually on the lookout for data from their studies that might provide clues to curing or minimizing the effects of cancer. I am no exception. Given what I'd learned about pyruvate in previous studies, I was hopeful that pyruvate could have an inhibitory effect on cancerous, or "uninhibited," out-of-control growths. You may be wondering what led me to think that pyruvate would have any effect on cancer or tumors. My explanation can be found in chapter 2.

Free Radicals, DNA, and Cancer

It is now believed by many in the medical community that cancer or tumors may be related to free radical production—short-term overproduction or consistent production through life. Exactly how they are linked is uncertain, but a popular theory is that free radicals, per se, damage your DNA. The damage to DNA, or its companion RNA, can lead to the production of a cancerous cell. These cells grow out of control, destroying the body as they expand in both size and numbers in a process that results in malignancy. Because I had already shown that pyruvate could control free radicals, and because I subscribe to the theory that free radical damage of DNA is a cause of malignancy, I decided to see if I could somewhat control cancer or malignancy by controlling free radical production with pyruvate. I went to work to test out my theory on a cancer or tumor.

When Downsizing Is a Good Thing!

I fed pyruvate or placebo to rodents prior to, and after implantation of, a breast tumor. At the end of the study, I analyzed the results and found that pyruvate seemed to slow tumor growth. Tumor growth occurred at the usual expected rate in those animals fed the placebo. Tumor size, weight, and metastases were reduced in those animals fed pyruvate (Figures 6.1 and 6.2 and Table 6.1). Further analysis showed that the DNA in those animals fed pyruvate was 40 percent less damaged than the DNA in animals fed the placebo (Stanko et al. 1994). I also discovered that while both sets of animals lost weight (an unfortunate side effect of cancer), the animals fed pyruvate experienced 40 percent less loss of body mass (mainly muscle) than those fed the placebo, suggesting that pyruvate inhibits muscle or protein loss when the body is experiencing stress, such as that created by malignancy (Stanko et al. 1994).

Although the results of this study were promising, one study wasn't enough. I went back a year later and did it all over again. The results were the same: Decreased tumor growth and greater body mass were found in those animals implanted with tumors and fed pyruvate than in those not fed pyruvate.

No News Is Good News

So my theory about inhibition proved correct. But how about prevention? Could long-term ingestion of pyruvate actually prevent tumors? Well, if you believe that DNA breakdown from exposure

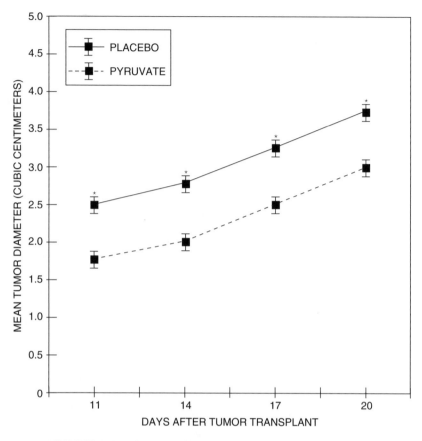

Figure 6.1. *Tumor size in animals fed the placebo or pyruvate.*

Source: R. T. Stanko, P. Mullick, M. R. Clarke, L. C. Contis, J. E. Janosky, and S. S. Ramasastry, "Pyruvate inhibits growth of mammary adenocarcinoma 13762 in rats," *Cancer Research* 54 (1994): 1004–7.

to free radicals can lead to tumors (and I do), and pyruvate inhibits free radicals, then by that logic, pyruvate could potentially be preventive. Of course, I probably won't know the answer—not in this lifetime anyway. Why? Because if taking pyruvate keeps you from developing a tumor, all you'll ever know is that you never got a tumor. You will never know whether you would have gotten one without taking pyruvate. To determine that would require long-term human studies of extraordinary magnitude,

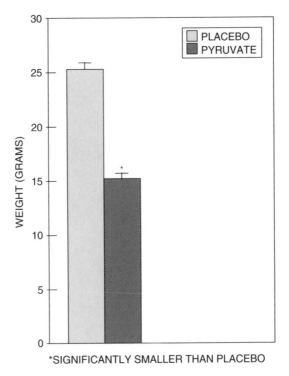

*SIGNIFICANTLY SMALLER THAN PLACEBO

Figure 6.2. *Final weight of tumor in animals fed the placebo or pyruvate.*

Source: R. T. Stanko, P. Mullick, M. R. Clarke, L. C. Contis, J. E. Janosky, and S. S. Ramasastry, "Pyruvate inhibits growth of mammary adenocarcinoma 13762 in rats," *Cancer Research* 54 (1994): 1004–7.

following thousands of controlled patients living under nearly identical circumstances for twenty or thirty years. In other words, it's not going to happen while I'm still alive! I also can't necessarily state that because pyruvate inhibited a breast cancer tumor, it would have the same positive effect on, say, skin cancer. Still, if the underlying cause of most malignancies is related to free radicals, as I believe it is, then pyruvate may well have an effect on any of those malignancies.

So pyruvate inhibits tumor growth and the DNA breakdown that many researchers feel is directly linked to tumor growth. In the war on cancer, pyruvate could be a very tough soldier.

Table 6.1. Microscopic Evaluation of Lymph Node, Liver, and Lung of Animals Transplanted with Tumor and Fed Placebo or Pyruvate

| | Percentage of Animals with Finding | |
	Pyruvate	Placebo
Lymph node tumor	85[†]	53
Lymph node necrosis	77[†]	40
Liver metastases	0	20
Liver cellular necrosis	0	33
Lung metastases (none)*	23	13
Lung metastases (1–10)*	62	60
Lung metastases (greater than 10)*	15	27

*Denotes number of metastases present in given microscopic section of organ
[†]In this tumor model, suggests trapping of implanted tumor in lymph nodes (a defense system against implanted tumor)

Source: R. T. Stanko, P. Mullick, M. R. Clarke, L. C. Contis, J. E. Janosky, and S. S. Ramasastry, "Pyruvate inhibits growth of mammary adenocarcinoma 13762 in rats," *Cancer Research* 54 (1994): 1004–7.

Q & A: Cancer

⌐?⌐ *Pyruvate hasn't been proved to prevent or treat malignancy. Shouldn't you wait to bring up the possibility that it might, until you've proved that it can?*

Speaking strictly scientifically, yes. I expect my scientific colleagues to question my hypothesis, which they should until all studies are completed. However, studies that might "prove" that pyruvate prevents or improves malignancy would take decades and would probably still be inconclusive. The type of long-term controlled human study necessary would be extremely difficult to conduct. Still, available data and common sense offer me enough information that I feel comfortable informing the public of this very exciting possibility. Remember, I'm not saying that pyruvate is a cure-all, or that it should replace traditional medical treatment for malignancy, or medical dogma. Taking pyruvate is not a license to indulge in high-risk cancer-causing behaviors such as smoking, poor diet, obesity, or excessive exposure to sun; nor should we think of pyruvate as the antidote to malignancy. I believe, however, that it can be a benefit as a component of a generally healthy lifestyle, one which may help keep the damage caused by free radicals and DNA breakdown at bay.

? *I've heard that other devastating diseases such as Lou Gehrig's disease and Alzheimer's disease have been linked to free radicals. Is that true, and, if it is, would pyruvate be useful in treating them as well?*

Yes and yes. Again, many competent, established researchers who have spent their lives evaluating diseases such as Lou Gehrig's disease (amyotrophic lateral sclerosis) and Alzheimer's disease feel strongly that these diseases are related to free radical–induced damage. A good review on Lou Gehrig's disease can be found in the January 26 issue of *Science,* "Mutant enzyme provides new insights into the cause of ALS," 1996.

Studies are currently being performed with a variety of antioxidants to determine their effectiveness in the prevention or treatment of these diseases, but the results are not yet available. As previously mentioned, there is growing scientific evidence that pyruvate inhibits progression of central nervous system diseases. I can, in good conscience (both scientific and personal), hypothesize and/or suggest that pyruvate could be beneficial in treating chronic degenerative devastating diseases, such as Lou Gehrig's or Alzheimer's disease. I am beginning studies that we hope and believe will verify that contention.

Anecdotally, a young woman with multiple sclerosis, a devastating disease of the central nervous system, reports that after taking 4 grams of pyruvate for four days, her ability to function after working eight hours as a nurse dramatically improved. She was able to clean her house, wash the clothes, and so forth, even without taking her interferon (for the record, I don't approve of her skipping her interferon), whereas before pyruvate she could barely master the ability to even drive home! I am glad for her because multiple sclerosis can be worse than debilitating, and I hope her improvement continues. I do, however, wish she would continue with her interferon!

? Isn't this chapter rather brief, since the prevention and treatment of cancer are such major goals in the world today?

It is brief, and it should be. Until I have further data to verify my thoughts and contentions, to write more would be irresponsible. In my mind, misleading the public and consumers is just as bad as, or worse than, withholding preliminary data. It is especially important not to offer false hope to anyone, whether an extremely vulnerable terminal patient or not. Far too often, misguided and desperate patients bypass accepted cancer therapy for the hollow "guaranteed cures" offered by offshore clinics or unproved alternative therapies. The results can be disastrous. In no way do I want pyruvate to be used in that type of amoral endeavor. I strongly support the policies of the traditional medical establishment in their efforts and treatments in the control of cancer. I do not recommend that cancer patients take pyruvate instead of visiting their oncologists, nor should taking pyruvate be a reason to dismiss early symptoms or warning signs associated with cancer. I stand very strongly behind the ongoing treatments of traditional medicine for malignancy.

? OK, we hear you, but could pyruvate be taken in conjunction with traditional cancer treatments?

Without a doubt, *yes*! Supplements, nutritional and otherwise, are not an uncommon component of accepted cancer treatment. And the many benefits of pyruvate, the effects on free radicals and DNA being the most promising, certainly might be beneficial to the cancer patient.

? Since my cancer diagnosis, I've lost quite a bit of weight. While pyruvate's benefits sound helpful for me, I'm concerned about its ability to promote weight loss, which would be the last thing I want now.

As I have discussed, pyruvate does indeed promote *fat* loss, by both inhibiting fat formation and enhancing fat breakdown. But, as might be expected, the greatest effects are found with excess body fat. Normal-weight people simply will not lose as much weight, if any, compared to someone who is obese. In my preliminary studies in animals that have a cancer, it seems that pyruvate enhances the stabilization of body weight and even increases body muscle and protein. Therefore, it would seem that the effects of pyruvate on body fat are controlled by your amount of body fat. Indeed, one of the subjects that I have anecdotally evaluated is a healthy woman whose natural weight is considered normal to somewhat below normal. While she's enjoyed other benefits of pyruvate, after several months of regular use, her weight has been unaffected. I have seen this with other effects of pyruvate. In patients with elevated blood glucose, pyruvate will lower the blood glucose. But in patients who have a normal blood glucose, pyruvate does not lower blood glucose levels. In ischemia, pyruvate inhibits free radical production, but not below what is considered a normal concentration. In patients with high blood cholesterol, pyruvate lowers blood cholesterol, especially in those patients on a high-fat, high-cholesterol diet. On the other hand, in patients with a normal blood cholesterol or those on a low-fat, low-cholesterol diet, pyruvate does not lower blood cholesterol. Time after time, I find that the effects of pyruvate on many metabolic parameters occur only if the parameter is abnormal. So, to answer your question, if you have a malignancy and you're losing body fat, it seems that pyruvate will not further promote fat loss. You might say that this sounds rather far-fetched, but a very commonly used medication—aspirin—functions in a similar manner. If you're running a temperature, aspirin will lower your temperature to normal; but if you're taking aspirin for its effect on the heart and you have a normal temperature, aspirin does not lower your temperature. Therefore, I don't believe pyruvate will further increase your weight loss, and it should be safe for you to take.

Q & A: Cancer

? *Could the effects of pyruvate on weight and exercise be beneficial in preventing malignancy?*

Yes. Many cancer experts feel that weight control and exercise, both improved with pyruvate supplementation, are involved in the prevention of certain cancers.

CHAPTER 7

Transplant: The Ultimate Ischemic Organ

No organ is more ischemic than one waiting to be transplanted. Completely cut off from any blood supply, a transplant organ could not be more vulnerable to cellular damage and death. If pyruvate could be beneficial in ischemia, I thought it would likely be beneficial for transplantation as well.

I was quite fortunate, at the time I decided to do this research, to have a veritable United Nations of top-flight researchers at the University of Pittsburgh: Abdul S. Rao, M.D., D.Phil., Director of the Transplantation Research Laboratory, from Pakistan; husband and wife Luca Cicalese, M.D., and Cristiana Rastellini, M.D., from Italy; Andre Borle, M.D., from Switzerland; and, of course, myself, from the United States.

I was also in the right place at the right time. My home base, the University of Pittsburgh, is one of the premier transplant centers in the world. One of the first liver transplant programs was established there, as was the new procedure, still being perfected, of transplant of the small intestine. The University of Pittsburgh also afforded me access to a great man, Thomas Starzl, M.D., the physician who first performed a liver transplant and whose words of wisdom were much appreciated.

I had three areas of interest: first, the newly developing technique of small intestine transplant; second, any potential that pyruvate might have for improving the well-established liver transplant; third, a very new and still experimental procedure, attempting to transplant islet cells (those cells which produce insulin) into diabetics who don't have functioning islets and, as such, cannot produce insulin on their own. I'll start with the most experimental of the three.

Inroads with Islets

Research on islet cells was conducted by Dr. Rao and Dr. Rastellini, who had been working with them for some time. The islet cells are the body's insulin producers, so the notion of being able to transplant them into diabetics is certainly an exciting one. It also is not easy, particularly because islets have a notable characteristic: The longer they can be preserved outside the body between the time they are extracted and the time they are transplanted, the more likely it is that they will not be rejected. Thus, the longer they are away from the body, the more they lose their antigenicity (their ability to stimulate rejection). Of course, the longer they're outside the body, the more likely they are to die. Perhaps even more to the point, the longer they're in storage, the greater the decrease in their ability to produce insulin. The trick is to find a way to store and preserve them outside the body in the best condition possible for the longest time possible, a problem which Dr. Rao and Dr. Rastellini had been working to solve long before joining the pyruvate research team.

To test pyruvate's effectiveness, Dr. Rastellini took a sampling of isolated islet cells; some were preserved in a standard solution, others in a standard solution containing pyruvate. The cells were then maintained for a varying number of days. During this time, she rendered a number of animals diabetic and transplanted the islet cells into them at various time frames to see if the cells made insulin. In each instance, the cells protected by pyruvate were more viable (Figure 7.1) and produced insulin. At the

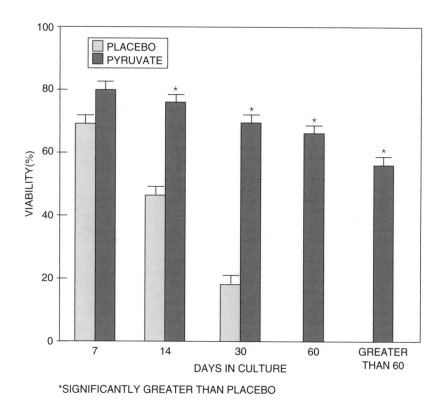

*SIGNIFICANTLY GREATER THAN PLACEBO

Figure 7.1. *Viability of human pancreatic islet cells in cultured placebo and pyruvate media.*

Source: C. Rastellini, L. Cicalese, A. Zeevi, C. Mattes, R. T. Stanko, T. E. Starzl, and A. S. Rao, "Long-term culture of viable human pancreatic islets in pyruvate-rich medium," *Transplantation Proceedings* 27 (1995): 3383–84.

thirty-day mark, those kept in regular solutions were just a little more than 20 percent viable, while those in pyruvate were nearly 80 percent so. At sixty days, when there were no viable cells remaining in the regular solution, those in pyruvate were still nearly 80 percent viable. While research is still under way, this suggests real hope for the eventual transplant of islet cells and the restoration of pancreatic function in diabetics.

So far, we were batting 0.333.

Intestine Testing

The next study involved small intestine transplant. This study was done by Dr. Cicalese, who had been researching this subject before joining the pyruvate team. Dr. Cicalese had already determined that one of the complications in transplanting a small intestine was, again, directly related to free radical production (Cicalese, Caraceni, Nalesnik, Borle, and Schraut 1996). Our testing of pyruvate's effectiveness in minimizing this problem was done in two parts.

First, we extracted small intestines from donor animals and stored them in one of two solutions, one containing pyruvate, the other not. We found, as had been the case in other studies, that those stored in pyruvate had a far lower free radical content than those stored in the other. We then placed pyruvate into those intestines and transplanted them into animals. Again, free radical production was decreased, and consequently the morphology (actual physical appearance) of the small intestine was far more normal in those animals who received the pyruvate-treated intestine than in those who did not.

Now we were batting 0.666.

Liver Transplant: Good, Could be Better

Having improved the chances of success with experimental and new procedures, I now wanted to see if an already well-established and successful procedure could get positive benefit from the addition of pyruvate. I chose to look at liver transplant, to see if we could improve a procedure in the same laboratories where it had been pioneered.

Working with animals, we perfused the liver with pyruvate before transplant, but we didn't stop there. After the transplant, the liver was infused with pyruvate through an intravenous catheter. There were two procedures and two very positive findings. If I simply perfused the transplant organ with pyruvate before transplant, there were benefits. However, those effects were far more consistent and profound if the organ was also perfused with pyruvate during transplantation.

What were the effects? The morphology of the transplant organ was greatly improved. There was a significant reduction in the number of inflammatory cells. Inflammatory cells are a major factor in the body's rejection of an organ, so decreasing them greatly improves the body's potential to accept the organ. Thus pyruvate helps maintain transplant organs outside the body (for example, during transportation) and helps in the body's acceptance of the organ.

Transplant: A Possible Scenario

Imagine that hepatitis has left you with a damaged and deteriorating liver. You're waiting for a transplant. While you wait, pyruvate supplementation helps keep free radical production down, potentially slowing your liver's deterioration and keeping you in the best condition possible for the transplant. Meanwhile, across the country, a liver becomes available. To keep it viable for as long as possible, it's placed in a pyruvate solution (to preserve its morphology) and rushed across the country.

Once the liver reaches the hospital, you're ready for the transplant. After the new liver is transplanted into you, it is again perfused with pyruvate, limiting the production of inflammatory cells and increasing the chances that your body will accept this life-saving organ.

So you see how a series of very separate research studies come together to possibly enhance the success of the miraculous procedure of transplantation.

We're batting 1000. That's not bad!

Can anybody bat over 1000? Before my research team presented me with the following data, I did not believe so. But I was wrong. We pretreated animals with pyruvate and placebo for one week. We then removed one of their kidneys while clamping off blood flow to the remaining kidney, to mimic the ischemia of the transplantation or severe operative ischemia.

After thirty-six hours all four of the animals treated with placebo were dead from kidney failure, while three out of four animals treated with pyruvate remained alive and well for three months!

If further survival studies of different ischemic conditions identify similar effects of pyruvate, pyruvate must be considered a *preconditioning* agent for transplantation or any surgical procedure. Moreover, in and of themselves, these preliminary data give further credence to the use of pyruvate for prevention of, or treatment for, any ongoing ischemic disease.

Q & A: Transplant

? *So, if I understand the chapter, you foresee that pyruvate could be used in a transport solution for donor organs?*

Without a doubt, it definitely could. I believe it could help to preserve the organs in better condition, for a longer time, between the time the organ is harvested and the time it is transplanted.

? *As a diabetic, I found your information on islet transplants very exciting! Can I, and other diabetics, expect to be able to undergo such a transplant soon?*

I wish I could say yes. However, even with the exciting strides we've made with pyruvate, islet cell transplantation by itself is fraught with difficulty and remains experimental in most cases. However, with people like you in mind, we'll keep trying to make this technique sounder. In the meantime, if the experimental treatment is the only one left available to you, I say, give it a try.

CHAPTER **8**

Vasodilatation and Nitric Oxide Production: More Interesting Than They Sound!

I'll be the first to admit it—the title of this chapter doesn't exactly make you want to rush home and start reading. But bear with me, because the information in this chapter offers some real clues as to why pyruvate has so many benefits and gives you some information on recent scientific discoveries that your doctor may not even be familiar with. So I will do my best not to bore you.

Pyruvate has been shown to induce vasodilatation and to increase production of inducible nitric oxide. Here's why that matters to you.

What Is Vasodilatation?

Vasodilatation is the dilatation, or expansion, of blood vessels. Its opposite is vasoconstriction—the constriction, or narrowing, of blood vessels. Perhaps the best way to indicate the potential benefits of vasodilatation is by describing the problems associated with vasoconstriction. Vasoconstriction raises blood pressure and decreases blood flow to organs. This decreased blood flow can result in ischemia and dysfunction of the organ deprived of blood flow, which might manifest in such ways as kidney dysfunction, cardiac dysfunction, leg ulcers, stroke, or impotency. Inducing vasodilatation in someone suffering the effects of vasoconstriction would, naturally, lower blood pressure and increase blood flow to organs, slowing or stopping the ischemic damage.

Increased Inducible Nitric Oxide Production Is Good Because . . . ?

First, let's congratulate nitric oxide. It was voted "molecule of the year" by *Science* magazine in 1992. Why? Because inducible nitric oxide has been determined to be one of the mediators of vasodilatation. In other words, if you stimulate inducible nitric oxide production, vasodilatation is one of the results. This is a real honor for a molecule which, up until a few years ago, was completely unknown. In fact, when I was in medical school, nitric oxide and free radicals had yet to be either discovered or understood. Your own doctor may not be familiar with the new research on the benefits of nitric oxide.

What do I mean by *inducible nitric oxide*? To make things a little confusing, our bodies house two kinds of nitric oxide. One is known as *constitutive* nitric oxide, which exists in our bodies at all times at a predictable level and promotes many functions of the body. The other is *inducible* nitric oxide, which is produced only as necessary. Increasing the production of inducible nitric oxide is very beneficial most of the time.

Pyruvate seems to promote the production of inducible nitric oxide, but its effect on constitutive nitric oxide has not been established. Therefore, it can promote vasodilatation, not to mention those other benefits associated with increased inducible nitric oxide production.

How did I find this out? It started with a study on blood cholesterol in 1989.

Lower Blood Pressure: An Unexplained Benefit

In this study, I evaluated a group of obese women on a high-fat, high-cholesterol diet, to see whether pyruvate supplementation would have any effect on their cholesterol levels, and indeed it did lower them somewhat. In the course of these trials, I monitored the women's vital signs, including blood pressure. When I evaluated all the data at the end of the study, I was surprised to discover that the women taking pyruvate had all experienced a small but significant drop in blood pressure (even the slightest blood pressure reduction can make a difference over time) (Stanko et al. 1992). Since the research community was still unaware of the potential benefits of nitric oxide, and since I had yet to prove pyruvate's ability to induce vasodilatation, I simply accepted this lower blood pressure as a positive effect that we couldn't explain at that time.

Dogged Research Pays Off

Move forward now to 1993, when I conducted heart research in dogs (see chapter 4). In that trial, I was able to precisely measure the effects of pyruvate and to show that it consistently, and effectively, induced vasodilatation (Figure 8.1). This solid evidence of pyruvate's ability to induce vasodilatation offers an explanation for the reduced blood pressure of the women several years before.

More Research, More Answers

In 1996, data from another test revealed still more information as to why pyruvate has such positive effects. In analyzing the data from my liver transplant study (see chapter 7), I found that pyruvate increased inducible nitric oxide production, probably secondary to the fact that it actually increased by fourfold the genetic material (messenger RNA) that signals the body to produce inducible nitric oxide.

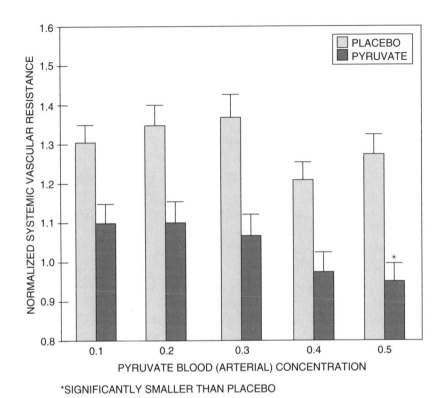

Figure 8.1. *Systemic vascular resistance in dogs receiving intraveous pyruvate or placebo.*

Source: J. Yanos, M. J. Patti, and R. T. Stanko, "Hemodynamic effects of intravenous pyruvate in the intact, anesthetized dog." *Critical Care Medicine* 22 (1994): 844–50.

What are the potential benefits of increased inducible nitric oxide production? In addition to the vasodilatation I've discussed here, it's quite a long list:

1. Neurotransmission
2. "Detoxify" free radicals
3. Destroy target cells, such as bacteria, viruses, tumor cells, and lymphocytes
4. Inhibit platelet aggregation and adhesion to blood vessels
5. Repair injured blood vessels
6. Regulate iron metabolism
7. Enhance penile erection (Billiar 1995)

The effects of nitric oxide certainly do parallel those of pyruvate. The relationship between the effects of pyruvate and nitric oxide metabolism is being vigorously evaluated in my laboratory and in others.

Q & A: Nitric Oxide Production and Vasodilatation

? *Given the information in this chapter, would pyruvate be beneficial in the treatment of hypertension?*

The effects of pyruvate on blood pressure are extremely small, and I personally have not convinced myself that it will be a consistent finding. On the other hand, the data are very convincing so far that pyruvate might slightly lower blood pressure; and remember, even a small drop in blood pressure over a long time is a major benefit in diminishing the complications of high blood pressure. Again, taking this natural metabolite shouldn't hurt you. If I had high blood pressure, I'd give pyruvate a chance.

? *You say pyruvate can't hurt, but I already suffer from low blood pressure and occasional resulting dizziness. Couldn't pyruvate make this problem worse?*

It shouldn't. Since the effects of pyruvate in decreasing blood pressure are small (5 to 10 percent), it is doubtful that it would have any noticeable or detrimental effect on your already low blood pressure.

? *I couldn't help but notice your brief mention of vasodilatation's association with erection. Are you suggesting that the increased vasodilatation induced by pyruvate might be helpful if I were to have problems getting an erection? Could pyruvate improve my situation?*

I've not done any studies on the effect of pyruvate on potency and arousal, and even if I did, studies would be difficult to control well enough to produce convincing data. But anecdotal reports—and I stress that these are anecdotal, uncontrolled reports of consumers taking pyruvate—suggest that while both men and women find that sexual arousal is unaffected by pyruvate (in other words, just taking pyruvate won't put you in a constant state of sensual excitement), sexual potency and/or stamina seems to be enhanced in some cases. These unscientific, uncontrolled personal reports would be consistent with the effect of pyruvate on vasodilatation, since vascular engorgement is a component of both male and female sexual stamina and potency.

? *I was reading about Viagra, and it seemed to me that it works in a similar way to pyruvate. Am I right?*

Essentially. Viagra, as we understand it, works by sensitizing the body to nitric oxide (in other words, it helps the body to better utilize the nitric oxide it normally maintains). Pyruvate, however, increases nitric oxide production. The end effect is the same: Enhanced access to nitric oxide equals increased blood flow, which leads to increased ability to maintain erection. Our anecdotal findings did, as we noted, suggest such an effect. Given the fact that pyruvate is totally natural, nontoxic, and without side effects, we think it's certainly worth a try, with or without Viagra.

CHAPTER 9

Anecdotal Findings

This chapter will not convince scientists, but it might stimulate them. The information that follows is not the result of clinical research or scientific trials. There have been no papers published and no trials conducted to back up what you'll read here. The information included in this chapter is what's known in the research field as *strictly anecdotal*—that is, information given to me by people who have used pyruvate. It relates their entirely subjective, purely personal description of the benefits they felt they received after using pyruvate. Much of what they say makes sense in light of what I, and others, have proved about pyruvate. Some of what they say may someday be investigated in clinical trials. Do not interpret the experiences related by our group of volunteers to be proof of the benefits of pyruvate; rather, consider them to be snippets of stimulating information.

If this isn't "proven" information, why am I including it? For several reasons. As I've stated many times in this book, some potential benefits of pyruvate would take many years to prove, if they could be proved at all. However, the anecdotal evidence is persuasive, and it makes enough sense in light of what we know about pyruvate that I think it's worth bringing to your attention. Additionally, you may experience some of these same benefits from pyruvate and wonder if you're imagining them, if they're a good or a bad thing, and if you're the only one to feel a certain way. This list covers some results that I've found to be relatively universal among those who have tried pyruvate. Finally, the anecdotal findings may become "proof" on the basis of future research.

Think of this chapter as a presentation of preliminary data. I'll relate what each subject thought were the benefits of taking pyruvate, followed by a list of findings present (or absent) in each individual.

In Their Own Words

D.L.: Female, age thirty-six, 5 feet 10 inches, 134 pounds, mother of one child, actor

D.L. had just moved to a new neighborhood and discovered that there was going to be a 10-kilometer run the following Saturday. Though a consistent runner, she'd been too busy to do any training, or even do more than a couple of trips to the gym, but she decided to make the run anyway. At this point, she had been taking pyruvate for five weeks. D.L. was stunned to discover at the finish that she had run her best time ever: 2.07 minutes faster than ever before. When asked if she felt a big difference while running, the answer was no, for the majority of the race. She still cramped up and experienced shortness of breath. However, she ran consistently until the end, when she felt a surge of energy that translated to an ability to run full out. This was a new experience, especially during the last 2 miles, when she says she picked up most of her time.

Aside from the successful race, D.L. noticed that she was less irritable and more able to tolerate the constant interruptions that go along with having a child. She experienced no high or kick from pyruvate, but did stop having the daily afternoon lull that usually made her want to take a nap at three o'clock. Her appetite diminished. Her sleep was deeper. Her already trim runner's legs were even slimmer than usual, particularly in the inner thigh area.

A.K.: Female, age thirty-six, 5 feet 5 inches, 114 pounds, businesswoman

A.K. works hard during the week and likes to go out and socialize with friends on weekends. At her size, it doesn't take much drinking to result in a hangover the next morning. While taking pyruvate, A.K. noticed that the morning-after hangovers were diminished. She was able to tolerate going for longer periods without food and not lose her strength or her ability to focus. A.K. experienced a weight loss of a few pounds, and cellulite disappeared. In general, she felt as if she were functioning as she had ten years before. A.K. also found the quality of her sex life improved; she was more aroused and involved, and more deeply satisfied.

R.A.: Female, age forty-eight, 5 feet 10 inches, 140 pounds, anesthetist

R.A. has a grueling job as an anesthetist. Her work starts at 4:00 A.M. and ends in the early afternoon. In addition, she runs 5 miles during her lunch hour in all weather conditions. By the time her day is over, she barely has the energy to drive home. However, once she started taking pyruvate, R.A. had some energy left for herself once she got home, without experiencing any "high" or "kick." During her noontime run, she found her ability to tolerate heat had improved. She lost a few pounds, along with cellulite. She slept better. At forty-eight years old, R.A. is experiencing an energy level she thought was gone for good.

B.S.: Male, age forty-nine, 5 feet 10 inches, 166 pounds, physician

B.S., no health-food fanatic, smokes more than even he knows is bad for him. On top of that, a busy schedule was keeping him away from the gym. After a few weeks on pyruvate, the slight paunch that had begun to develop disappeared. His appetite was diminished, and the beginnings of cellulite went away. His skin was clearer, and the irritation generally caused by smoking had all but disappeared. He was less anxious and angry about daily activities and less bothered by stressful business negotiations. While working, he found himself better able to focus. An avid golfer, B.S. went from tiring on the sixteenth hole to finishing eighteen, ready to play another round. All in all, B.S. felt considerably younger than his forty-nine years. He also noticed that the benefits disappeared after stopping pyruvate.

L.O.: Female, age thirty-five, 5 feet 6 inches, 120 pounds, writer

L.O. had gained some pounds over the holidays and had lost most of them, but she was stuck at the last few pounds that would have returned her to her preholiday weight. She started taking pyruvate but was busy on a book project, so she didn't start the exercise she had planned. In fact, long hours resulted in her adding a little pizza to her usually healthy diet. To her shock, her already reasonably flat stomach became defined, her thighs became thinner, and, most exciting, cellulite visibly diminished. Although she comes from a slender family, they're very thin-skinned, and even her 98-pound mother has cellulite, so this was a real thrill. Next, she noticed that her allergy symptoms were reduced. This was most striking when, after an hour of being around a friend who smokes, she realized she wasn't sneezing and itching, a condition that usually begins after five minutes around cigarette smoke. The occasional redness and dry patches caused by allergies, cigarettes, and the dry Los Angeles air all but disappeared. Even her boyfriend noticed the quick improvement. She was able to sustain household chores longer, still able to get things done at a point when she would normally have been worn out. As a writer, she usually has a number of stories roaming around her head and has trouble falling into a deep sleep. She also has more than her share of nightmares. After taking pyruvate, she slept better, and even her dreams were far more pleasant. She awoke feeling more refreshed than she had for some time. She was rebounding from food, stress, and environmental conditions as she did when she was in her twenties.

R.M.: Male, age forty-six, 5 feet 10 inches, 162 pounds, script analyst/theatrical instructor

When he started on pyruvate, R.M. was entering a busy period of preproduction for directing a college theatrical event as well as teaching classes, and he feared he was about to come down with a serious flu. Happily, he didn't get sick. He also found, in spite of a huge increase in activity, that he was calmer and better able to focus than he had been. His appetite decreased, and he slept more soundly but for fewer hours.

N.S.: Female, age thirty-three, 5 feet 6 inches, 116 pounds, beautician/exercise instructor

Because of medication sensitivity, N.S. only took $1/2$ to 1 gram of pyruvate per day. She immediately noticed sounder sleep, increased exercise capacity, and more energy to work and do household chores. She rode her bicycle farther and with less strain. She was less irritable with her son. Even given this small dosage, she noticed that these benefits were gone after stopping pyruvate.

With more than 5 million patient doses of pyruvate ingested by consumers prior to the publication of this book, I could go on and on with these personal reports of the benefits of pyruvate. I have received more than 250 to 300 personal reports similar to the ones just cited. It is doubtful that such consistent findings in a small group of subjects will disappear in a larger group, so I'll stop with these. I do stress, however, that with all the doses of pyruvate consumed and personal reports received, none has been associated with adverse side effects.

Benefits: An Overview

These benefits will probably be universal:

- Increased energy
- Ability to work better
- Ability to exercise longer
- Smaller thighs
- Calm, less irritable disposition
- Increased concentration

These benefits are to be expected:

- Sounder sleep
- Increased well-being
- Flatter abdomen
- Noticed difference after stopping pyruvate
- Decreased appetite
- Decreased allergic symptoms
- Sensation of feeling young again

These benefits will probably be experienced by many:

- Difficulty finishing a meal
- Ability to eat without gaining excessive weight

Some benefits might occur, or might not:

- Decreased cellulite
- Better heat tolerance
- Improved skin

It's doubtful that these benefits will occur; consider them "maybes":

- Increased sexual stamina
- Decreased hangover

The following benefits are not to be expected:

- Sensation of "kick" or "jolt"
- Lost abdominal roll

Summary of Anecdotal Reports

1. Women and men respond the same.
2. A dosage of 3 to 5 grams per day is adequate.
3. Findings are consistent with effects of pyruvate on energy production, fat metabolism, cardiac function (blood flow), and free radical production.
4. There is seemingly selective loss of body fat in abdominal and thigh fat deposits.
5. The effects on the central nervous system (brain), while not unexpected, are surprisingly consistent. They could

be secondary to energy production, blood flow, nitric oxide production, or free radical metabolism.

6. Effects are seen within forty-eight hours of consuming pyruvate and are conspicuously absent within 48 hours after discontinuing it. Although no "rush" or "high" is appreciated while consuming pyruvate, subjects actually noticed that effects disappeared when not consuming pyruvate.

7. There is no such entity as cellulite. Loss of "cellulite" reported by subjects is consistent, though, with loss of subcutaneous fat in thighs. Irrespective of what I call it, subjects felt their thighs, buttocks, and abdomen "looked better" with loss of "pocks," "divots," "bumps," or "holes," referred to by most as cellulite.

8. Reports of decrease in appetite are surprising but consistent. There is no explanation at present.

Q & A: Anecdotal

? *Quite a few of the subjects in these anecdotes were already at what most of us would consider a desirable level of weight and fitness when they began taking pyruvate, yet they went on to lose 1 to 1½ pounds in the first week or so of taking pyruvate. Would they continue to lose weight, and in fact become underweight, if they continued taking pyruvate?*

It's doubtful. Here's why. First, even though you may think someone's in perfect shape, most of these people probably have a spare pound here or there which would account for that initial loss. Beyond that, my follow-ups have indicated that weight loss stops once that minimal "extra" poundage is eliminated. Any weight loss that I have identified in slender people has also been "selective," that is, weight loss in the thigh or stomach areas that store extra fat as opposed to all-over weight loss. This distinction is vital, because continued, all-over weight loss (loss of both fat and muscle mass) can lead to malnutrition, while selective weight loss (fat only, muscle mass remains constant) only attacks extra fat. While this sounds too good to be true, it precisely mimics my earliest findings in human and animal studies: Most weight loss was fat, and muscle mass remained relatively constant. Actually, percentage of body mass increased, while percentage of body fat decreased. This intriguing finding has been verified by other independent investigators in controlled outpatient studies. The effects of pyruvate on fat and muscle parallel my findings concerning blood pressure and blood sugar levels: Pyruvate seems to act as a stabilizer. So pyruvate seems to drive fat, muscle mass, blood pressure, blood sugar, and so forth, toward normal levels. Is this explicable? Not currently. Is it good for you? Yes!

[?] You have a chapter on heart and energy and one on endurance. All your subjects seemed more energized and had increased exercise capacity. Are the two benefits related?

They could be related, but there is reason to believe that two different mechanisms are involved with increased energy and increased endurance after pyruvate consumption. Both mechanisms benefit us together, but my guess at present is that they probably act independently.

The increased energy in the cells is biochemical in nature. Pyruvate changes certain metabolite ratios which, through normal metabolism, leads to increased baseline energy in the cell (see chapter 4). This increased energy will be present whenever you take pyruvate, irrespective of the fuel demands of exercise. This energy can explain the energized feeling and the increased ability to perform daily activities that our subjects reported, which incidentally has been identified by other investigators.

Enhanced endurance with pyruvate is probably related to increased glycogen (fuel) stores in the body and increased uptake of glucose (fuel) by exercising muscles. The relationship of this increased exercise fuel, which also occurred at baseline before exercise, and increased baseline cellular biochemical energy is not yet established.

[?] *You say that your subjects slept more soundly, felt more alert during the day, and (some) had a decreased appetite after taking pyruvate. Does this suggest that pyruvate has an effect on the brain or central nervous system?*

It's entirely possible that the energy stores of the central nervous system are higher while a person is taking pyruvate. Pyruvate is also known to be involved in the excitation-transmission signal between independent brain cells that results in normal function. As I've previously mentioned, scientific evidence is accumulating that pyruvate protects against certain central nervous system abnormalities. Therefore, it is not unexpected that some central nervous system effect would occur while taking pyruvate. However, it's surprising that the effects were so universal and seemingly beneficial in this group of disease-free, mostly younger subjects. Taken together, preliminary data would suggest beneficial effects of pyruvate on the central nervous system, but now we need more investigations to determine the exact mechanisms of these benefits.

[?] *While the initial effects of taking pyruvate seem beneficial, I wonder if they would diminish (or maybe increase) without altering the dosage?*

I simply cannot be sure at present. It will take further investigation (and quite some time) to accurately answer this question. There seems to be, though, a peak level of effects reached after a couple of weeks. This would suggest that my recommendation— using pyruvate at therapeutic doses for eight to ten weeks, decreasing (or stopping) the dose for one to two weeks, and increasing or restarting—would be an effective and safe dosage schedule. As I've mentioned previously, I recommend that you take pyruvate for an extended period in order to derive the expected long-term benefits on the heart (and other organs, including the brain) and on free radical production, as well as other beneficial effects (such as fat and weight control) which must be long-term. The dosage schedule given above would seem to be ideal. However, it's important to emphasize that even if you find that you have an increase in exercise capacity of 50 percent by taking pyruvate at therapeutic doses for six weeks, you will not increase it by 100 percent by continuing pyruvate at these doses for twelve weeks unabated. After all, even a superathlete can do only so much! However, very preliminary, anecdotal data suggest that once you do decrease, then increase the dosage of pyruvate, all the benefits previously realized recur and could be additive over time.

⟨?⟩ *Do you have any anecdotal or personal reports of the use of pyruvate for pets or other animals?*

I have an interesting report from Carl Coppolino, M.D., of Nutripharm Health Resources in Tucson, Arizona. Dr. Coppolino was approached by a horse trainer who was entering a 1200-pound Arabian horse in a coast-to-coast endurance race and requested nutritional supplements for training the horse. Dr. Coppolino supplemented the horse's diet with pyruvate, extrapolating dosage from our human dosage schedule. The horse won the endurance race! This story is very uncontrolled and anecdotal but exciting and stimulating nonetheless.

CHAPTER 10

RTS Pyruvate

The Pyruvate Start-Up

Before this book went to press, pyruvate products had already appeared in the marketplace. You might have seen the magazine advertisements, the flyers, or our coverage in the media. Maybe one of those is what led you to buy this book. Thanks to this early press, the initial interest in pyruvate has been exceptionally strong.

Unfortunately, some of the product on the marketplace was not that of RTS Industries and Pharmaceuticals, and the complaints I received inspired this section of the book. It is designed to inform you about our pyruvate project company structure, our standards of quality, and what to look for when you buy pyruvate.

The road to creating a quality product—one that's efficacious, safe, scientifically credible, at a cost that's not prohibitive to the customer but allows enough profit for the company to grow—was neither short nor easy. The wild and competitive nature of the supplement trade meant that, on top of everything else, I was constantly concerned with unscrupulous patent infringers.

However, given the choice between getting product on the market sooner or getting product on the market correctly, there was no choice. When it comes to both corporate and personal goals, RTS Industries, our independent quality control company, and our suppliers are in total agreement concerning efficacy, safety, and scientific credibility. We will not compromise these things.

Ensuring the Purity of RTS Pyruvate

While the bulk of this book is dedicated to telling you about the benefits of pyruvate, this section sounds a note of caution. RTS Industries and our strategically aligned business partners SKW, Ellis Foods, Ellis-Arnold Laboratories, and Lunden own almost all the pyruvate patents for production and use; but intense consumer interest in pyruvate has spawned, not unexpectedly, unlicensed (infringer) or "black market" pyruvate products. The scenario is this: With only profit in mind, disreputable producers take advantage of the overwhelming demand for pyruvate product by selling hastily made, inferior product with the "take the money and run" attitude. They brazenly sell this essentially illegal (unlicensed) product, banking on the fact that we won't find out and that if we do, we won't want to get into the costly and time-consuming process of an infringement lawsuit. Regardless of the fact that most infringers have no concern for the products' efficacy or safety, they can keep us tied up in court for years, arguing their right to sell inferior product. Such is the nature of business today. I, and others, have taken the time and expense to obtain patent protection for our discoveries, and companies have contracted for these rights through licenses. Infringers (those without a license for this patent protection) are simply stealing the lifelong efforts of prestigious scientists and businesspeople for their own undeserving use and financial gain. This is done with product that doesn't work because it wasn't made properly in the first place and probably doesn't even contain much pyruvate, and so they are stealing from the consumer also.

The RTS trademark and apple logo are the symbols which promise the product you buy has undergone extensive testing and measures up to my exacting standards. Frankly, RTS Industries is one of the few companies in the supplement industry that has its own independent quality control and tracking. When you buy a pyruvate product, look for the RTS name and the apple logo. One of them will appear on all our products and on those of our licensed distributors. This name and logo indicate that these products have been subject to, and meet, the strict standards of quality and efficacy that I have established for pyruvate. If the RTS or apple logo is missing from any pyruvate product, I cannot stand behind the product and suggest to you that it might not be beneficial or even safe, and should be avoided.

The 85-percent Solution

Pyruvate has a lot of things going for it, but it tends to be a little unstable. If you don't treat it right, it falls apart. To benefit from pyruvate, our scientists feel that the product you take must contain at least 85 percent pure pyruvate. It must also be manufactured in such a way that the level of purity stays almost constant throughout its shelf life. If made improperly, the pure pyruvate level is low to begin with and then deteriorates further (and fairly rapidly) as it stays on the shelf longer, leaving you with side product and filler and little active pyruvate. Some of the infringer products we evaluated contained as little as 2 percent pyruvate, and the filler (98 percent of the capsule) could not be accurately defined.

Keeping an Eye on Infringers

How did we find out about the problems? Our attorneys and others monitored the market constantly. I began to get phone calls from people I'd never met, complaining that pyruvate was not what I said it was. Although I was able to explain to the callers that they were getting unlicensed product, I continue to be concerned about those who made their judgments about pyruvate based on an inferior (in some cases nearly nonexistent) "pirate" pyruvate product. I tracked down some infringer product, and Figure 10.1 shows you the contrast between RTS pyruvate product (manufactured by SKW) and some of the pirate pyruvate samples we found. The infringer graph shows a number of peaks, indicating impurities, and the content of pyruvate is much lower.

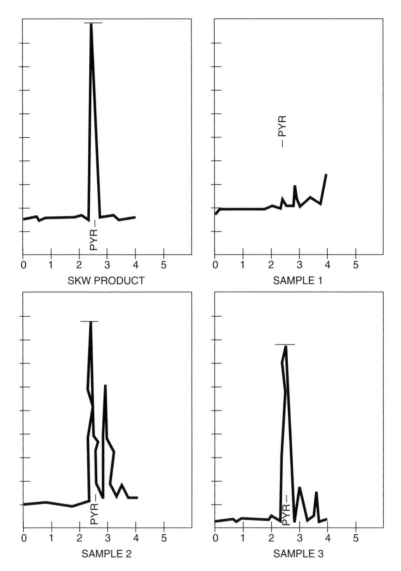

Figure 10.1. *Evaluation of pyruvate content of SKW product and infringer products.*

Analyses of SKW product show one peak of calcium pyruvate in high concentrations. Other products show either small amounts of calcium pyruvate (sample 1) or lower amounts of calcium pyruvate with other peaks of organic compound contaminants (samples 2 and 3).

Note: Simplified for presentation.

CONCLUSION

Twenty-five years of academic research usually result in voluminous data, graphs, ideas, hypotheses, and potential; and as you have just read, my studies on pyruvate were no exception to that rule. It seems that pyruvate offers some benefits for almost everyone. These benefits were identified as they should be, and need to be: through peer-reviewed, double-blind university studies, most of which are verified by more than one prestigious scientist. As far as I am aware, this is a first for any dietary supplement.

As the United States begins to accept (albeit with skepticism) that supplements can provide long-sought-after benefits, these findings, and the manner in which they were discovered, are reassuring. Certainly drugs provide life-saving benefits for many. However, traditional medicine is now expanding to consider the benefits of supplements, especially in the area of prevention. Prevention and long-term proactive therapies are the bywords for improved health in our nation.

Drugs come with a disadvantage for long-term treatments: The potential for serious side effects is magnified by long-term or preventive use. Supplements, with minimal side effects, are seemingly ideal, however, as a preventive or well-being treatment. My data suggest that pyruvate, always in our body and diet, is a prime example of an ideal in such a scenario.

Excess weight and obesity are rampant in any prosperous, highly developed, and industrialized society. The ammunition against excess weight, dietary restriction, exercise, and metabolic control of fat metabolism are all improved by pyruvate, so much so that prevention of excess weight, certainly a national goal, should be easier to accomplish.

Exercise has myriad benefits for maladies other than obesity, including diabetes, hypercholesterolemia, heart disease, lung disease, vascular diseases, and even cancer. Pyruvate will increase our exercise capacity. It also improves diabetes and blood cholesterol all on its own.

Heart disease is a major killer in the world. Pyruvate protects against ischemic heart disease, and it also makes the heart more efficient, powerful, and energized. It's hard to believe you could derive so much benefit to the heart from a natural compound, but many, many studies suggest it's so.

Free radicals, the chemical bad guys that have been identified only in the past twenty years, cause myriad acute diseases, chronic diseases such as Alzheimer's disease, and all ischemic diseases, as well as diabolically causing us to age. Long-term control and prevention of free radical formation are imperative. No other nontoxic compound has been shown to inhibit the production of the mother of all free radicals: superoxide. Only pyruvate performs this vital service. However, pyruvate doesn't stop with inhibition. Pyruvate keeps on working to scavenge any free radicals it missed to begin with. What more could you ask for?

Protection of DNA and inhibition of cancer growth—these are not minuscule goals. When it comes to accomplishing them, pyruvate seems to star again! It helps you sleep more soundly, work harder, and do so more efficiently. But pyruvate can't turn back the clock, so that you could have started taking it at an earlier age. It can, however, make you feel as if the clock has been turned back. Add protection of the eye as another plus for pyruvate.

Last, but far from least, the University of Pittsburgh has pioneered organ transplantation under the direction of great and talented physicians, and it appears that pyruvate might enhance even their extraordinary accomplishments.

Concluding Thoughts

I'm writing this during my weekly flight from Pittsburgh to our offices, production plants, and quality control facilities in California. As I fly over the Rocky Mountains, I can't stop analyzing the voluminous data that my decades of research on pyruvate have generated and remembering how difficult it was for me to initially believe the incredible results we continued (and still continue) to find. We generated data like my laboratory findings that pyruvate, a simple three-carbon compound always present in our bodies and diet, protects DNA; the results were so incredible that I repeated the studies, with consistent results. Even then, it was only when I heard Dr. Rolf Bunger speak about his findings that pyruvate protects lymphocyte DNA against damage, findings corroborated by his multiple studies, and by my own, that I allowed myself to accept these findings as real. His studies on isolated hearts, which confirmed pyruvate's ability to enhance cardiac efficiency and pumping; studies in Germany showing that pyruvate improves heart function in humans; and others were further cause for overall confidence.

With any new compound, skepticism will exist, especially among scientists. Almost all scientists are skeptics; they wouldn't be scientists if they weren't always questioning. I welcome constructive questioning. My own questioning led to new findings concerning the beneficial effects of pyruvate. In the supplement arena, usually devoid of reproducible data, no other compound has been as extensively evaluated as pyruvate. The reproducible findings concerning the benefits of pyruvate from multitudes of prestigious scientists in different academic institutions provide an armamentarium to move pyruvate from evaluation in the ivory-tower laboratory and research center to therapeutic supplementation for the health of the general public.

I am finally, scientifically, convinced that pyruvate can provide many, many benefits to society. It is gratifying to me that enhancing metabolism with natural compounds might influence acute and chronic disease, as it is the only way I feel we can do so both effectively and safely. Certainly prevention is the best way to control any disease, ranging from obesity to heart disease. I usually do not like to use the term *well-being agent*. Besides having a subjective meaning, in the past, these types of compounds have been associated with charlatans, money grabbers, false promises, and no research. However, if any compound were ever to be credibly identified with some confidence as a well-being agent, pyruvate certainly deserves to be so identified.

The thrill of scientific discovery is overwhelming. I recognize that I have played only a small part in the discovery and identification of a new, safe manner of potentially improving health. Still it is thrilling to be a member of a team that seems to have achieved this primary goal of all dedicated scientists and physicians.

In the meantime, I can enjoy the multitude of benefits afforded to me by pyruvate, and now so can you!

APPENDIX

Pyruvate in Foods

Most foods contain a low level (less than 25 milligrams per serving) of pyruvate. Of forty different foods evaluated for pyruvate content, none of the foods was completely free of pyruvate. Certain foods have a rather high level of pyruvate: fruits, vegetables, cheeses, beer, wines, and fermented foods. The minimum daily intake of pyruvate in the average industrialized diet is probably about 0.1 gram (100 milligrams), with the average intake probably about 0.5 to 1 gram per day. To put this into perspective, the dose necessary to cause the beneficial effects of pyruvate identified in studies is around 3 to 5 grams per day. Consequently, to obtain these benefits, pyruvate supplements will need to be taken, or pyruvate can be added to certain foodstuffs, drinks, bars, and so forth. These products will be available to the consumer at about the time of publication of this book.

Pyruvate is approved at present as a flavor enhancer to be added to foods. From 10 to 50 milligrams of pyruvate is probably found in the average diet as a flavor enhancer. As such, the Flavor and Extract Manufacturers Association has designated pyruvate as *generally recognized as safe (GRAS)* when added to specific foods at very low dosages (parts per million).

Amount of Pyruvate Present in Foods

Food	Pyruvate per serving
Cheddar cheese	13 milligrams per 4 ounces
Provolone cheese	50 milligrams per 4 ounces
Emmentaler cheese	122 milligrams per 4 ounces
Red apple	450 milligrams per 8 ounces
Golden Delicious apple	155 milligrams per 8 ounces
Grape juice	36 milligrams per 8 ounces
Banana	80 milligrams per 4 ounces
Red onion	17 milligrams per ounce
Spinach puree	72 milligrams per 4 ounces
Garlic powder	150 milligrams per ounce
Beer	70 milligrams per 12 ounces
Red wine	70 milligrams per 6 ounces

As you can see, if you calculate the amount of food you'd need to consume to ingest 3 to 5 grams daily of pyruvate, supplementation with pyruvate is imperative. At less than 0.5 gram of pyruvate per red apple, for example, you'd need to consume approximately six to ten red apples each day just to get your pyruvate. Besides the inconvenience of this regimen, you also add calories that you probably do not need. However, do I recommend choosing pyruvate-rich foods when you have the option? Of course I do.

REFERENCES

The Alpha-Tocopherol Beta Carotene Cancer Prevention Study Group. 1994. "The effect of vitamin E and beta carotene on the incidence of lung cancer and other cancers in male smokers." *The New England Journal of Medicine* 330: 1029–35.

Behal, R. H., D. B. Buxton, J. G. Robertson, and M. S. Olson. 1993. "Regulation of the pyruvate dehydrogenase multienzyme complex." *Annual Review of Nutrition* 13: 497–520.

Billiar, T. R. 1995. "Nitric oxide: Novel biology with clinical relevance." *Annals of Surgery* 4: 339–49.

Borle, A. B., and R. T. Stanko. 1996. "Pyruvate reduces anoxic injury and free radical formation in perfused rat hepatocytes." *American Journal of Physiology* 270: G535–40.

Bunger, R., R. T. Mallet, and D. A. Hartman. 1989. "Pyruvate-enhanced phosphorylation potential and inotropism in normoxic and postischemic isolated working heart." *European Journal of Biochemistry* 180: 221–33.

Cavallini, L., M. Valente, and M. P. Rigobello. 1990. "The protective action of pyruvate on recovery of ischemic rat heart: Comparison with other oxidizable substrate." *Journal of Molecular and Cellular Cardiology* 22: 143–54.

Cicalese, L., P. Caraceni, M. Nalesnik, A. Borle, and W. H. Schraut. 1996. "Oxygen free radical content and neutrophil infiltration are important determinants in mucosal injury after rat small bowel transplantation." *Transplantation* 62: 161–66.

Cicalese, L., K. Lee, W. Schraut, S. Watkins, and R. T. Stanko. 1996. "Pyruvate prevents ischemia-reperfusion mucosal injury of small rat intestine." *American Journal of Surgery* 171: 97–101.

Cortez, M. Y., C. E. Torgan, J. T. Brozinick, Jr., R. H. Miller, and J. L. Ivy. 1991. "Effects of pyruvate and dihydroxyacetone on the growth and metabolic state of obese Zucker rats." *American Journal of Clinical Nutrition* 53: 847–53.

Cross, C. E., B. Halliwell, E. T. Borish, W. A. Pryor, B. N. Ames, R. L. Saul, J. M. McCord, and D. Harman. 1987. "Oxygen radicals and human disease. Davis Conference." *Annals of Internal Medicine* 107: 526–45.

Deboer, L. W. V., V. A. Bekx, L. Han, and L. Steinke. 1993. "Pyruvate enhances recovery of rat hearts after ischemia and reperfusion by preventing free radical formation." *American Journal of Physiology* 265: H1571–76.

Epstein, F. H. 1997. "Antioxidants and atherosclerotic heart disease." *The New England Journal of Medicine* 337: 408–16.

Gaziano, J. M. 1998. "When should heart disease prevention begin?" *The New England Journal of Medicine* 338: 1690–91.

Ivy, J. L., M. Y. Cortez, R. M. Chandler, H. K. Byrne, and R. H. Miller. 1994. "Effects of pyruvate on the metabolism and insulin resistance of obese Zucker rats." *American Journal of Clinical Nutrition* 59: 331–37.

Kanter, M. 1995. "Free radicals and exercise: Effects of nutritional antioxidant supplementation." *Ex Sport Science Review* 23: 375–97.

Lasley, R. D., R. Bunger, Z. Zhou, and R. M. Mentzer. 1994. "Metabolically based treatment of stunned myocardium." *Journal of Cardiac Surgery* 9: 469–73.

Mallet, R. T., and R. Bunger. 1993. "Metabolic protection of postischemic phosphorylation potential and ventricular performance." In *Interactive Phenomena in the Cardiac System*. Edited by S. Siderman and R. Beyer, pp. 233–41. New York: Plenum Press.

Melanson, K. J., E. Saltzman, R. R. Russell, and S. B. Roberts. 1997. "Fat oxidation response to four graded energy challenges in younger and older women." *American Journal of Clinical Nutrition* 66: 860–66.

"Mutant enzyme provides new insights into the cause of ALS." 1996. *Science* 271: 446–47.

Rastellini, C., L. Cicalese, A. Zeevi, C. Mattes, R. T. Stanko, T. E. Starzl, and A. S. Rao. 1995. "Long-term culture of viable human pancreatic islets in pyruvate-rich medium." *Transplantation Proceedings* 27: 3383–84.

Robertson, R. J., R. T. Stanko, F. L. Goss, R. J. Spina, J. J. Reilly, Jr., and K. D. Greenawalt. 1990. "Blood glucose extraction as a mediator of perceived exertion during prolonged exercise." *European Journal of Applied Physiology* 61: 100–5.

Salahudeen, A. K., E. C. Clark, and K. A. Nath. 1991. "Hydrogen peroxide–induced renal injury. A protective role for pyruvate in vitro and in vivo." *Journal of Clinical Investigation* 88: 1885–93.

Sohal, R. S., and R. Weindruch. 1996. "Oxidative stress, caloric restriction and aging." *Science* 273: 59–63.

Stanko, R. T., and S. A. Adibi. 1986. "Inhibition of lipid accumulation and enhancement of energy expenditure by the addition of pyruvate and dihydroxyacetone to a rat diet." *Metabolism* 35: 182–86.

Stanko, R. T., and J. E. Arch. 1996. "Inhibition of regain in body weight and fat with addition of 3-carbon compounds to the diet with hyperenergetic refeeding after weight reduction." *International Journal of Obesity* 20: 925–30.

Stanko, R. T., T. L. Ferguson, C. W. Newman, and R. K. Newman. 1989. "Reduction of carcass fat in swine with dietary addition of dihydroxyacetone and pyruvate." *Journal of Animal Science* 67: 1272–78.

Stanko, R. T., H. Mendelow, H. Shinozuka, and S. A. Adibi. 1978. "Prevention of alcohol-induced fatty liver by natural metabolites and riboflavin." *Laboratory Clinical Medicine* 91: 228–35.

Stanko, R. T., A. Mitrakou, K. Greenawalt, and J. Gerich. 1990. "Effect of dihydroxyacetone and pyruvate on plasma glucose concentration and turnover in non-insulin dependent diabetes mellitus." *Clinical Physiology and Biochemistry* 8: 283–88.

Stanko, R. T., P. Mullick, M. R. Clarke, L. C. Contis, J. E. Janosky, and S. S. Ramasastry. 1994. "Pyruvate inhibits growth of mammary adenocarcinoma 13762 in rats." *Cancer Research* 54: 1004–7.

Stanko, R. T., H. Reiss Reynolds, D. Lonchar, and J. E. Arch. 1992. "Plasma lipid concentration in hyperlipidemic patients consuming a high-fat diet supplemented with pyruvate for 6 weeks." *American Journal of Clinical Nutrition* 56: 950–54.

Stanko, R. T., R. J. Robertson, F. L. Goss, R. J. Spina, J. J. Reilly, Jr., and K. D. Greenawalt. 1990. "Enhanced leg exercise endurance with a high-carbohydrate diet and dihydroxyacetone and pyruvate." *Journal of Applied Physiology* 69: 1651–56.

Stanko, R. T., R. J. Robertson, R. J. Spina, J. J. Reilly, Jr., K. D. Greenawalt, and F. L. Goss. 1990. "Enhancement of arm exercise endurance capacity with dihydroxyacetone and pyruvate." *Journal of Applied Physiology* 68: 119–24.

Stanko, R. T., G. Sekas, I. A. Isaacson, M. R. Clarke, T. R. Billiar, and H. S. Paul. 1995. "Pyruvate inhibits Clofibrate-induced hepatic peroxisomal proliferation and free radical production in rats." *Metabolism* 44: 166–71.

Stanko, R. T., D. L. Tietze, and J. E. Arch. 1992a. "Body composition, energy utilization, and nitrogen metabolism with a 4.25 MJ/d low-energy diet supplemented with pyruvate." *American Journal of Clinical Nutrition* 56: 630–35.

————. 1992b. "Body composition, energy utilization, and nitrogen metabolism with a severely restricted diet supplemented with dihydroxyacetone and pyruvate." *American Journal of Clinical Nutrition* 55: 771–76.

Stephens, N. G., A. Parsons, P. M. Schofield, F. Kelly, K. Cheeseman, M. J. Mitchinson, and M. J. Brown. 1996. "Randomized controlled trial of vitamin E in patients with coronary disease: Cambridge Heart Antioxidant Study (CHAOS)." *The Lancet* 347: 781–86.

Whitaker, R. L., J. A. Wright, M. S. Peke, K. D. Seidell, and W. H. Piety. 1997. "Predicting obesity in young adults from childhood and parental obesity." *The New England Journal of Medicine* 337: 864–73.

Willet, W. 1997. "Weight loss in the elderly: Cause or effect of poor health?" *American Journal of Clinical Nutrition* 66: 737–38.

Yanos, J., M. J. Patti, and R. T. Stanko. 1994. "Hemodynamic effects of intravenous pyruvate in the intact, anesthetized dog." *Critical Care Medicine* 22: 844–50.

INDEX